MADAME PRIME MINISTER

Madame

Books by Emmeline Garnett

MADAME PRIME MINISTER
 The Story of Indira Gandhi

TORMENTED ANGEL
 A Life of John Henry Newman

SEASONS: A CYCLE OF VERSE
 An Anthology

AN ARIEL BOOK

Prime Minister

THE STORY OF *Indira Gandhi*

by Emmeline Garnett

 FARRAR, STRAUS & GIROUX | NEW YORK

"It is a question of being a human being, not a man or woman."
—Indira Gandhi

Contents

Acknowledgment

This book has been compiled from many sources, mostly from printed books and newspapers (see bibliography, page 141). I am grateful for personal help from the office of the Indian High Commissioner in London, from staff and pupils present and past of Badminton School, and in particular for a great deal of help from Marie Seton, a close friend of Indira Gandhi and the author of a book on Jawaharlal Nehru* which she generously allowed me to see and make use of before publication.

* *Panditji* by Marie Seton (London: Dennis Dobson; 1967).

MADAME PRIME MINISTER

Madame Prime Minister

The date was January 11, 1966, and the Prime Minister of India had just died in a foreign country, in circumstances which were both tragic and romantic. The tragic element was that he died after less than two years in office, just long enough for a country which desperately needed good statesmen to find out that they had probably got one. The romantic element was that he died a martyr, an entirely twentieth-century martyr to the demands of statecraft. The ink was hardly dry on the signatures to a difficult and much needed treaty, when Lal Bahadur Shastri died of a heart attack brought on by the strain of negotiating it.

His coffin was loaded on to a blue and silver aircraft by a President and a Prime Minister, and when it flew into New Delhi his countrymen flocked out in emotional millions to weep for him. A little to their own surprise they discovered how much they had loved and

trusted the sparrow-like little man. Their love and respect were made greater when it was revealed that the
sixty-one-year-old Prime Minister had nothing to
show for thirty years of political life but a small bank
overdraft. It could happen only in India. His family
did not even own the roof over their heads.

Next day a million people watched the flames rise
from the pyre of sandalwood logs by the sacred river
Jumna, and when nothing was left but ashes India
turned to its own problems again, the most urgent of
them all being, "Now who?"

To go back a while: India had gained her independence from Britain only eighteen years before. At that
time, unable to agree on mutual tolerance within the
same federation, the Moslem states of India had set up
on their own as Pakistan, the Hindu states had remained as India. The results of this partition were
measured in human suffering. For although a state
might belong predominantly to one or the other religion, the population of the subcontinent was then, and
still is, inextricably mixed. At least fourteen million
people migrated to get on the side of the border that
seemed to offer safety—Hindus into India, Moslems
into Pakistan. Their fears were well-founded. A wild-
fire of riots and civil strife ran through the states, and
perhaps half a million people died, at a reasonable guess,
of murder or the diseases that follow refugees.

But individual human problems and tragedies aside,
the worst political problem left by partition was the
state of Kashmir in the northwest. Its allegiance has

never been settled. It has been on the agenda of the Security Council at the United Nations since 1948, to no avail. Pakistani and Indian troops glare at one another across the cease-fire line, and every so often the four million Kashmiris break out into violence. Sometimes police action has been enough to quell the troubles, sometimes troops have been needed. In August 1965 the boat was rocked once too often, and the result was a border war between India and Pakistan.

Time was when neighbor states could fight to a finish over disputed frontiers, without the whole world biting its nails and wondering who else would be involved. Not any more. As Indian troops drove across the cease-fire line, the big powers were looking more than anxious. China had her own quarrels with India and might side with little Pakistan. And if that happened, the United States . . .?

It was Russia which took decisive and valuable action. The Prime Minister of India and General Ayub Khan, the President of Pakistan, were invited to Tashkent, a Russian city not far over the Kashmir border. There the Russian Prime Minister Alexei Kosygin managed to get an agreement between the two countries. Not a direct agreement over the future of Kashmir; but he persuaded the two leaders to sidestep this central problem and at least agree to withdraw their opposing troops behind the old cease-fire line and exchange their prisoners of war. It was something—more than had looked possible a few months before.

The signing, on January 10, 1966, was duly cele-

brated by a banquet, and the newspaper correspondents
noted that Mr. Shastri, who had worked like six beavers
over the negotiations, looked tired but content. Cameras
clicked and flashed, registering smiles on every face.
The Russian vodka flowed, but Mr. Shastri drank his
toasts in sips of orange juice and soda water. The cameras clicked again, as everyone shook hands; the tiny
Prime Minister came up to nobody's shoulder, his hand
was almost lost in the large military grip of General
Khan. "This is a good agreement," he said.

At half past one in the morning he staggered from
his bedroom, coughing and clutching his heart. Seven
minutes later he was dead.

And after Shastri, who? It was ironical that two
years earlier the problem had seemed just as acute.
Then it had been "After Nehru, who?" Or even, "After
Nehru—what?" as though, when that great leader died,
the floods would rise and drown India's struggles
toward a stable democratic economy.

India is an underdeveloped country politically as
well as economically. It does not have a crowd of
reasonably capable statesmen able to take over in an
emergency. The rulers and their administration have
not yet had time to develop a tradition of ruling.
Eighteen years is not a long experience, and before that
their youth was spent in British jails, or in more or less
open rebellion. The administration is inexperienced and
therefore open to corruption. At the same time no country can produce the totally incorruptible, the saints of
politics, more naturally than India. There are always

some of them around, the Gandhi-like figures who refuse to grow up into the sophisticated ways of the world, who make a private sense of rightness and honor serve them in public too. Shastri was one of these.

There is a poem by Rabindranath Tagore in which someone asks what will happen when the sun sets. There is silence in the falling darkness until an earthen lamp says quietly: "Light me: I will do the best I can." After the sun of Jawaharlal Nehru set, for a year and a half Lal Bahadur Shastri provided a warm, patient little flame which his country came to value more and more. He did not try to flare very high, but he set himself quietly to deal with one problem after another near to the ground.

But India's problems are vast and it sometimes seems insoluble. First, foremost, and all the time, there is the poverty of her people. Poverty, malnutrition, ignorance, disease make the Indian's expectation of life the lowest in the world. It has risen by five years of late, but still stands at about thirty-two, less than half that in the Western nations (in the United States it is seventy). And yet, in spite of this cruel death rate, India's population adds to itself by four or five million extra mouths a year. India has nearly 500 million people, with not enough to eat, still mainly living in villages, tied to the land at bare subsistence level. A small minority has imagination, education, and experience enough to see that conditions can be improved. To see that you can escape means that you are halfway out of the hole and can already breathe fresher air.

Many of India's millions are still shackled by tradition: "Thus it has always been, no good will come of change."

And yet there should be a way out, for India is potentially a rich country even if her people are poor. Peasants scratch for a living over the top of huge deposits of iron ore, coal, and most if not all of the minerals for modern industrialization. Oil is being discovered. Billions of tons of spare water power thunder down from the mountains and run off to the sea. And there is enormous, though primitive, man power—"a hundred million men with teaspoons," as somebody said about China. One day perhaps all these reserves will be effectively harnessed.

But will anybody ever succeed in harnessing the castes and creeds and cultures into a working team? India speaks in fifteen main languages and a hundred and twenty minor ones. Although most of its people are Hindu, there are still nearly fifty million Moslems, not to mention ten million Christians and millions of Sikhs and Buddhists and Jains. From time to time violent disturbances break out here or there—disturbances over religion, over language and culture (the warlike Sikhs of the Punjab claim a separate state like Pakistan); disturbances for sheer hunger (the state of Kerala is rationed to one cupful of rice per person per day).

Basically the troubles all have the same roots: people like things the way they are, they value their own way of life and don't want to be pushed around. But how can you legislate for the development of India without pushing someone? And there is always the problem of Kashmir, the problem of Pakistan. On the north and northeast broods the threat of China, pushing farther, marking out a boundary which eats southward into India's mountains.

Not enough food, not enough money, not enough experienced administrators, too many people, powerful and covetous neighbors, restlessness among the minorities, illiteracy and backwardness and superstition. And then Shastri, who seemed a small miracle in the desolation after Nehru's death, was himself dead. What now?

And the answer to that "What now?" holds a special interest for the Western countries, which in this respect are more tied by the chains of tradition than India. A woman president is still unthinkable in Washington or Paris. There are queens in England and Holland, but in both these countries a woman prime minister, the executive who actually leads the government and makes the decisions, is just as unthinkable. But it was a woman prime minister, Indira Gandhi, who emerged from the Congress Party's voting after Mr. Shastri's death.

"I do not regard myself as a woman. I regard myself as a person with a job," she answered the inevitable first question at her first press conference.

We may feel surprise and admiration, however. For in India there is still the total seclusion of women, which is called purdah, there is still the courteous silence of women, who eat only when their husband has finished, there are still arranged marriages and all the paraphernalia of apparent inequality. And yet the road is open to women as it is not in Western nations.

India has produced the first and only woman president of the United Nations General Assembly. Congress, in India, has four times had a woman president. There have been two women state governors, and many women ministers at state and federal level. In the two houses of the central government there are more than fifty women members—about one in fifteen, which is not equity yet, but about the same proportion as the British House of Commons has managed in the forty-odd years since it first admitted women members. Moreover, the leader of the docker's union in Calcutta and the head of the railway workers' union have both been women—unthinkable in any Western country.

Indira Gandhi's election produced more questions from the foreign correspondents than from the Indian ones. How could she do it? Would she be strong enough? How would she manage her male colleagues? Most important of all, had she been elected because she was the daughter of Jawaharlal Nehru, darling of his country? Could she have anything to offer of her own?

This last question was not fired at her in press conferences, but it was bandied around in private more than any other. And no one knew the answer. No one, it was discovered, knew Indira Gandhi.

They knew her from the outside. No one was more easily recognizable than the slim imperious figure in the beautiful sari with the white goose wing in her dark hair. (She reminded one reporter of a Hapsburg princess, he said rather nervously.) Her face, sad, almost tragic in repose, would suddenly lighten in a smile that charmed even her opponents. To hear her talk, you felt that she was saying all she thought, without reserve. And yet, when on this important day people tried to sum her up, to guess the future, she was essentially cool, remote, and totally unknown.

True, she could hold a mass audience as nobody had been able to but her father, but could she hold the crumbling Congress Party? She had been a good president of Congress, but was that by accident or by force of the prestige of being the third generation of her family? She had often shown courage in going straight to the center of disturbances or riots, but had she any ideas of her own with which to solve the problems behind these disturbances? She had refused several times in the past to be urged toward the job she now held—was that lack of ambition, or weakness, or a preference for power behind the scenes, or what? Nobody knew. Perhaps she did not know herself. "Did I want this job or did I not?" she said to a friend. "I don't know—you tell me."

The fortunes of 500 million people fell into the hands of Indira Gandhi on January 19, 1966. This story tells something of how she came to be where she was on that day. History will tell how she carried the burden that came to her then.

Founders of the Family

Allahabad is a city with its feet rooted firmly in history. It sits on the beak of land formed where two of the seven sacred rivers of India meet and join together, the blue-gray Jumna and the Ganges tawny with silt. Some say that a third invisible river, the Saraswati, flows in between the others to make up a three times sacred confluence. Every year for three thousand years, at the festival of Magh Mela, thousands of pilgrims swarm into Allahabad to bathe and pray at this holy place.

Much that has happened to Allahabad has happened because of its rivers. When there are few roads in a country, and those few liable to be washed out because of monsoon rain, a place on a river is important because of the ready-made highroad past its door. A place on two rivers is better still. It cannot help but grow and prosper.

10

Allahabad, moreover, has associations with the
Ramayana (the story of Rama), one of the great
Indian epic poems. On the fourth day of his exile,
Rama came to Allahabad. And fourteen years later, on
his return, he was met there by his faithful half
brother Bharata. This is rather like saying that your
home town is built on the site of Abraham's camp, or
the precise spot where Moses saw the burning bush.

In later times, the Grand Trunk Road came to Allahabad, halfway along its fantastic length from Calcutta to Peshawar. Anyone who has read *Kim* remembers the romance of it. "And truly the Grand Trunk
Road is a wonderful spectacle. It runs straight, bearing
without crowding India's traffic for fifteen hundred
miles—such a river of life as nowhere else exists in the
world."

Later still came the railway-building age, and again
Allahabad was a convenient junction. All the time the
city grew, until it was the tenth largest in all India. As
it grew more prosperous, people gathered to it, and on
one of the waves of history there drifted in a family
called Nehru.

They had not always been called Nehru. They had
lost their family papers but kept in their family memory the fact that they had come down from Kashmir
two hundred years before. Indeed, they carried the
stamp of their origin in pale complexions and delicately
boned features. From Kashmir's high green valleys and
snows ("Learning, lofty houses, saffron, icy water and
grapes: things that even in heaven are difficult to find

are common there") they had migrated to Delhi, scholars in the court of one of the Mogul emperors. Somewhere along the way they adopted the name of Nehru, which was first a kind of nickname because they had a house alongside "nahar," the canal.

The Moguls declined in power as rulers of India, and their place in the complex of history was taken by the East India Company of England. Then, in the course of time, the East India Company was, so to speak, nationalized, and the British government took over—a process that someone once described as "acquiring an empire in a fit of absent-mindedness."

In the middle of the nineteenth century the Nehrus of Delhi were scholars, lawyers, police officers—nothing very fancy, but they were sufficiently well-to-do and well in with the powers that ruled them. The Nehru boys were even learning a little English along with Sanskrit and Persian. Since the British raj was apparently here to stay, it would be useful for ambitious young men to know the language.

In 1857 Northern India was convulsed by the Indian Mutiny, now also called the First War of Independence. As usual, the innocent suffered the most; with a hundred and fifty thousand other refugees, the Nehru family left Delhi, which the victorious English were plundering savagely in retaliation. Over the next few years the Nehrus drifted eastward along the Grand Trunk Road, from Delhi to Agra, from Agra to Allahabad.

It was a largish family group, what in India is called

a "joint family." This means that sons and the wives of sons, unmarried daughters, grandchildren, sometimes cousins to the second and third degree, all live under the same roof. The head of the Nehru family at the time it settled in Allahabad was Nand Lal, a moderately successful lawyer in the High Court; one of his cares was his youngest brother Motilal, born after their father's death, in 1861.

They settled in the old city of Allahabad, which under British rule was now the provincial capital of the United Provinces. Its seething narrow streets lay on one side of the railway tracks, and on the other side, up a slight hill where the air was a little fresher in the summer heat, were the Civil Lines, the neatly laid out bungalows, four to a block, of the British civilians, punctuated by so many churches of so many Christian sects that one might have though Allahabad to be a sacred city of the Christians rather than the Hindus.

But not only churches were built. There was a movement for better Indian education, and in Allahabad, about the time the Nehrus went there, the foundations of the Muir Central College were laid. It was designed to grow into the University of Allahabad. Today it has nearly ten thousand students, but it began modestly enough in 1872 with thirty-five boys in the first year of high school. Motilal Nehru joined it in the fourth year after its opening.

The principal was an imposing gentleman called Augustus Harrison, who, almost hidden behind a waterfall of beard, rode a large tricycle around the college grounds, greeting everyone with a hearty "Well, my boy!" or, if it were a less friendly occasion, with "I shall fine you heavily, very heavily, say—one rupee!" His students loved him. They knew he bought them prizes out of his own pocket, and they suspected that he subsidized students who could not pay the fees, also from his own pocket.

There was no difficulty about the fees for Motilal Nehru, for Nand Lal's legal practice flourished extremely, but like many others Motilal Nehru had reason to remember Principal Harrison very kindly, and he kept a rubbed and folded letter from his teacher until he himself was an old man.

The affection was returned. Motilal was a born leader. First in the paper-pellet battles at which Mr. Harrison smiled inside his beard ("We can put up with incompetent or lazy boys but not with dishonest ones"), then as star of the cricket team, introducer of the rather new and very European game of tennis, energetic, charming, and quick-witted, Motilal climbed straight to the top of the school in everything but marks.

He lost marks not through stupidity but because he was too busy doing other things. Until he was twelve he had been taught only the traditional Persian and Sanskrit (equivalent to the traditional curriculum, in European schools, of Latin and Greek), and he did not speak any English. But once he started to learn the things he wanted to learn, he wasted no time. English was one of the things he wanted to learn. It was the language of the raj, of power and progress.

The elder brothers had had an impressive lesson in the usefulness of English, on the road out of Delhi, before Motilal was born, in the heat of the Mutiny. Their little sister, very fair even for this Kashmiri family, and probably crying in the misery of the hasty evacuation, was mistaken for a kidnapped English child and the family was stopped by English soldiers with harsh words on the edge of turning to blows. Many Indians had been strung up to the nearest branch of a tree before they had had time to explain themselves. Luckily, though, Nand Lal and his brother spoke enough English to put things right. The language of the raj was indeed a useful skill.

But Motilal grew up, it seems, with no bitter family memories of the Mutiny days. Of course he was a nationalist—they were all nationalists, although the term wasn't in use—but the way ahead lay up the British ladder of success, and he genuinely admired the British way of life. Muir College inspired no more violent nationalistic feeling than a desire to beat the European Boys' High School at cricket.

At this time, true Indian nationalism was conservative. Those who aspired to a truly Indian society could only look backward to what had been in the past, and what had been in the past was the unchallenged rule of a society that had got itself knotted up in a web of caste.

Caste is more easily explained than understood. "A caste," says a modern writer on India, "is a group of families whose members can intermarry and eat together without being polluted. Each caste, each group,

has a particular place on the social ladder. Above and
below it on the other rungs are a long series of other
groups, other castes, just as in a ladder each step has its
place." This social organization provided complete
security, but in return for the security every trivial
action of life was regulated, there was no breaking out
of the position into which one was born. And over the
years the four main castes and the fifth group, the
outcastes, had split and resplit into thousands of subcastes. "In Western terms," says the same writer, "the
subcastes made about as little sense as if the drivers of
single-deck buses were born into a trade union so exclusive that the drivers of double-deck buses had to eat
in a separate canteen, wear different uniforms, and be
debarred from marrying into the families of single-deck
bus drivers."

British rule had offered some slight loosening of this
paralysis. It had brought some equality into the administration of law, and had banned certain practices, in
particular suttee, the death by burning of a widow on
her husband's funeral fire. So it was not surprising that
in the 1870's and 1880's, in a peaceful, comparatively
forward-looking town like Allahabad, the new Indian
middle classes saw hope for themselves through Westernization. High starched collars, coats and waistcoats,
pin-striped pants, and polished shoes were the signs of
modernization.

The yellow and white tower of the new university
on the hill represented Western education opening up

for Indians. In theory it had long been held that all
Queen Victoria's subjects were equal. "No native of
India by reason only of religion, place of birth, de-
scent, colour, or any of them, would be disabled from
holding any office or employment." In practice it had
been very difficult indeed for Indians to compete. If
they wanted to join the Indian Civil Service it meant
education in England, and few cared to undertake this
when it would leave them socially outcast on their
return, not properly accepted by the Westerners, re-
jected by their own people.

Now it was slowly becoming easier. There were
more families like the Nehrus, who cared little for
breaking with Hindu tradition. (At least the men cared
little, though the women were more conservative.) They
were ready to cross the sea to Europe, to send their sons
to Oxford and Cambridge. When they returned, it did
not matter if some members of the community frowned;
there were enough of them to make up their own
community.

Motilal Nehru, however, blundered at the very beginning of his career. When he came to sit for his
university finals at the city of Agra, he was so dis-
gusted with his first paper (it was English) that he
walked out and spent the rest of the exam sessions
admiring the Taj Mahal.

The incident seems out of character. He was an
ambitious and intelligent young man. Never again in his
life, as far as one can see, did he give up like that at the

mere smell of danger. Perhaps he had been careless and overconfident and this failure gave him a salutary jolt. Perhaps there was a more personal reason. Like most Indians, he had been married very young, and his girl-wife and their new-born son died together. The dates are uncertain, but if this personal tragedy coincided with the end of his studies, it might well have made him, for the moment, sick of living.

Whatever the reason, having failed to take his B.A., he pulled himself together in time. There were not so many educational chances for Indians that anyone, muffing one of them, could expect a second. A law career provided one of the most hopeful openings for clever Indian boys. Motilal decided to follow his elder brother, Nand Lal, into the courts. He worked diligently and came out this time, in the law exams, at the top of the list with a gold medal. At the age of twenty-two he went to nearby Cawnpore to work for three years as a kind of legal apprentice. At twenty-five he came back to join his brother's practice and to marry again.

Then he received a blow that might have been the end of his ambitions. Nand Lal died suddenly in mid-career, and Motilal found himself the head of a family: a young wife, his mother, sister-in-law, two nieces and five nephews, with himself the only breadwinner.

Now all the energy he had was channeled into a driving ambition. He would get on. He must, and he did. No doubt there were helping hands waiting to give him a boost for his brother's sake, but Motilal had considerable gifts of his own. His first brief brought in exactly five rupees, but after that, advance was swift.

He had a profusion of gifts; knowledge came easily to him, and as an advocate he had the art of presenting his case in its most attractive form. Every fact fell into its proper place in the narration of the story, and was emphasized in just the right degree. "He had an exquisite public-speaking voice and a charm of manner which made it a pleasure to listen to him." So said one contemporary. Another said: "Pandit Motilal was handsome. He dressed fastidiously. He was by no means eloquent, but keen in debate and incisive in argument. He radiated cheerfulness and good humour . . . While Pandit Motilal was in the court and on his legs, the atmosphere seemed charged with sunshine."

The sun shone warmly on his home life too. His second marriage was to a charming little china doll of a bride just past her fifteenth birthday, a fair child from another Kashmiri family, cream-skinned, hazel-eyed, with brown hair which brushed below her knees when it was allowed to fall loose. At first the sunshine was not quite so bright for Swaruprani as it was for Motilal, though. With a dashing husband she had also acquired a tartar of a mother-in-law, fiercely possessive over her darling youngest son. It must for a while have been tough going for Swaruprani, who had herself always been the spoiled center of attention. The youngest and most beautiful of three sisters, she had been brought up by the eldest, ten years older than herself. In the sad custom still prevailing at this time, this eldest sister had

been a child bride and had been widowed while still a
child, which meant complete renunciation, a shaven
head, and a plain white sari for the rest of her days.

As a social habit, this waste of a young girl's life can
hardly be defended. But like many things that are bad
in theory, it could work on individuals who accepted it,
wholly for good. Bibi Amma, as she was known in the
Nehru family until, her life's work over, she died with
quiet determination twenty-four hours after her beloved Swaruprani, was so nearly a saint that no one
would have had things different.

Swaruprani soon had the son that she and Motilal
longed for. He died. Then she had another son, whom
they called Jawaharlal—the Red Jewel—a name he
detested and would have changed if he could.

In his two marriages, Motilal had altogether four
sons, of whom three died in infancy. The love lavished
on an only son in India can hardly be exaggerated, but
in this case it was underlined by those three deaths.
The survivor was even more precious. Certainly it was
said of Motilal in years to come, when his fame as an
Indian leader was second only to that of Gandhi, that
much as he loved India it was only an extension of his
love for his son.

The sun continued to shine. By the time he was
forty, Motilal's income was almost outrunning his
power to spend it, and that was saying something. He
marked his increasing Westernization by a visit to
England and then, on his return, by a refusal to go
through the purification ceremony which the strict

Kashmiri Brahmans said was necessary. "Tomfoolery," snorted Motilal Nehru.

The day came when the family moved out of the old city and across the railway tracks to the Civil Lines and a smart European-type bungalow. The fees continued to roll in and now the first house was not good enough for a man with Motilal's expensive and hospitable habits. They moved again, to a new district beyond the university. Motilal bought a really enormous house, derelict and rambling, but with a huge garden, two swimming pools, and great possibilities. "Anand Bhawan," he called it: "House of Happiness."

By the time it was finished, it was the finest house in Allahabad, and Motilal lived in it like the prince he was. The story has been often told and as often denied that he sent his shirts to a laundry in Paris. It is worth repeating simply because people felt that it ought to be true of a man with Motilal's wealth and exuberance.

There was electric light and superior plumbing—neither of them common luxuries. There was an Indian dining room and a European dining room. There were beautiful books and pictures, china and glass, food and wine. Motilal went to London every three or four years now, and while he was there he spent his money richly, bringing back treasures for Anand Bhawan.

As far as he could be, he was the complete English gentleman. His children had English tutors and governesses. Even, at one moment, the edict went forth that the household would speak nothing but English. (An appalled silence followed, since most of the women had

not an English word between them.) Motilal's suits and
hats and shoes came to him from London's most exclusive makers. His watch chain and his mustache would
have been happily at home in the House of Lords. The
first automobile in Allahabad belonged to him—who
else? Later he had two cars at a time and a stable full of
superb horses and carriages as well.

Among the family photographs there is an endear-
ing one of Motilal at the wheel of a magnificent and expensive car. The date is about 1904. He is wearing a flat
yachting cap (the whole idea of driving in those far-
off times was adventurous, rather like putting out to
sea). The spare tire, carried on the roof, looks very
much like a lifebelt put there in case anyone should
fall overboard. The coachwork shines like black por-
celain, a turbaned attendant stands by, the two little
Nehru daughters, beautifully ribboned, look out of the
windows. This is the picture of a very successful man.
Looking at it, you can imagine Motilal about to break
into that famous laugh which echoed down the veran-
dahs and through the lofty rooms of Anand Bhawan—
the laugh of a man who had got what he wanted by his
own efforts, who was pleased with himself, with his life,
with his family and friends, and saw nothing ahead of
him but sunshine and smooth water.

Jewel of the Nehrus

Another family photograph from the Nehru album: father, mother, and the five-year-old son in his glory. Jawaharlal wears a sailor suit, a velvet sailor suit, a successful cross between the British navy and little Lord Fauntleroy, long stockings, boots, Eton collar and flowing bow tie. He also has, but invisibly, a large silver spoon in his mouth.

Behind him stands his father, conscious of two kinds of success: the success of profession, money and status on the one hand; on the other the success, more important to him, of having fathered the proud child perched on the chair at his feet. Beside them both the beautiful, delicate Swaruprani sits on a couch, in rich silks and jewels, but pale and serious with the absorbed look of someone who is often ill. When the picture was taken, she was only in her midtwenties, but already looks worn by ill health. She had never been quite well since

Jawaharlal's birth. They all got used to the fact that Mother needed more care and attention than anyone else in the household.

Childhood was a lonely time for Jawaharlal in spite of the swarming Indian family household with its cousinhoods, its comings and goings, and its crowded servants' quarters. The cousins were too much older to be playmates, and the Nehru children came so spaced out that each in his or her own way was an only child. Jawaharlal's sister (Nan to the family, Mrs. Vijayalakshmi Pandit to the world at large) was eleven years younger than he, and the second daughter, Krishna, seven years younger than Nan. Somewhere in the middle came another son who died within a month of his birth. By the time Jawaharlal married and had a daughter, his younger sister, Krishna, was ten years old, and so Indira too was an only child. In all the splendor of Motilal's household there was always a lonely child.

Little Jawaharlal emerged briefly into the outside world at the age of seven, when he spent six months in the baby class of the local convent school with a cousin of the same age. But the cousin was only on loan while his parents were in Europe. When they returned, the cousin went home again, and Motilal had now risen to such eminence that he preferred private tutoring for his son.

So Jawaharlal's education was carried on at home, with English tutors and English governesses. English was his first language and probably always his best—

at least, years later a companion in prison said that Jawaharlal talked in his sleep in English. As he grew up, he read Dickens and Scott and H. G. Wells, *Sherlock Holmes* and *Tom Sawyer* and *The Prisoner of Zenda*, like any boy of any English-speaking country from a middle-class home.

But it was also the home of Swaruprani, who spoiled him ("I knew that she would condone everything I did"). On the women's side of the house, everyone spoke Urdu or Hindustani, all was delicacy and scented silk and the pungent good smells of Indian cooking. Here he heard the endless stories from the epics, which his mother and Bibi Amma knew almost by heart, the *Ramayana* and the *Mahabharata*. It was pleasant to go, hand in hand with his mother or his aunt, to dark and incense-smelling temples, but it was the half-shamed pleasure of a boy playing with dolls. He knew that really he belonged to the men's world, where these things did not count. Mubarak Ali, his father's Moslem clerk, told him more realistic stories of the Indian Mutiny, blood-curdling and true, for Mubarak Ali's father had been hanged by the British while his mother looked on.

From behind the curtain at the dining-room door Jawaharlal observed his father and the cousins and their friends. Sometimes someone saw him there, and Motilal called him in and set him on his knee, an eminence the little boy did not really like, as the talk rolled and thundered in the cigar smoke over his head. Sometimes there were English people at dinner, valued

friends of his father's. Yet sometimes Jawaharlal heard
stories, particularly from one of the more muscular
cousins, of overbearing British behavior, of clashes in
railway carriages, where the two peoples could not help
meeting, and sometimes of insults and blows. In fact, he
was absorbing a dual attitude toward the raj, a love-hate
relationship that was more easily felt than explained.

There were occasional family vacations—not many,
though. Motilal's work in the High Court was demand-
ing. It brought the rupees rolling in, but they rolled
out again just as generously, and to talk of saving, or of
living below his income, seemed vaguely insulting to
Motilal, as though his capacity for earning as much as
he ever wanted were in doubt. Still, there were occasions
when the family went away together—never as far as
Kashmir, though it was in their bones to go back some
day, but to nearer hill country, Mussoorie perhaps,
where both British and Indian well-to-do families went
in the summer to escape the worst of the hot weather.
One would leave the sweltering plains and after a long
hot train ride emerge so high above the heat line that
there would be fires lit in the evening and blankets on
the beds.

When he was seven, on one of these trips Jawaharlal
saw a glacier for the first time. The boy from the
dusty plains never forgot the thrilling sight. Often in
the long stretches in prison when the heat was un-
bearable, he thought of that glacier. Once he wrote to
his sister, urging her to take her young sons to see it as

soon as she could, because it would be an unforgettable experience for them, as it had been for him.

Jawaharlal loved both his parents. ("I admired father tremendously. He seemed to me the embodiment of strength and courage and cleverness.") They adored him in return, but on occasion he was witness to Motilal's temper. It was a royal, superb temper which could break up parties, but it was a generous temper, too, the roaring of a lion at the head of his pride. Those of his family who did not inherit it imitated it. Jawaharlal met it physically only once. He was about five at the time, and he "borrowed" a fountain pen from his father's desk (well, nobody could want *two* pens, could they, not even Father?). He remembered the occasion all his life, long after the sore places had been soothed away by his mother's sympathy and cold cream.

Motilal had been several times to Europe alone, but in 1905 the whole family set off in first-class style. Motilal, Swaruprani, Jawaharlal, and little Nan. The object of the journey was to leave Jawaharlal at an English school, but it was also a splendid holiday trip, as everything was splendid in Motilal's company. He was so much larger than life. Once he had passed, people on ships, people in hotels and stores remembered him for a long time. Stories circulated and sometimes came back to other members of the family years later.

Who but Motilal would have had the idea of celebrating Nan's birthday (they were in a German hotel at the time) by inviting four hundred local schoolchil-

dren to tea? Discipline went with the luxury, though.
Five-year-old Nan, looking like a doll princess in her
ribbons and flounces, rings and necklaces and bangles,
was sent around the whole four hundred to shake hands.
Behave like royalty and you get taken for royalty.
Motilal was tickled by the inaccurate but flattering
stories that were told about him.

Jawaharlal was left at Harrow, to wear a straw boater
and learn the intricacies of this exclusive private school
misleadingly called, in the English fashion, a public
school. He was fifteen, a smallish pale boy, gentle,
sensitive, intelligent, holding himself very erect, self-
sufficient, wary, and much more sophisticated than
English boys of his age. In any case, he was two years
older than most of the other new boys, and had been
lucky to find a place at all, but Motilal was persuasive
and his money and prestige spoke up too. Like the
German hotelkeeper, the English vaguely assumed that
all rich Indians were princes at least, and space can be
made for a princeling where there is none for ordinary
mortals.

It was by now fashionable for rich and progressive
Indians to have their sons educated in England; there
were four or five others contemporary with Jawaharlal
at Harrow. And these Indian schoolboys gave rise to a
folklore figure in boys' magazines. School stories of the
time often include an Indian prince whose English is
funny but whose heart is in the right place, and who
is amazingly generous with cash. His father might
have been Motilal, who wrote to his son: "Make

many friends . . . occasionally entertain them on holidays and half-holidays . . . patronize the creameries
. . . never mind the expenses which cannot be very
great." And he wrote again, obviously longing to hear
that Jawaharlal had been in a real fight. "Please do not
suppress the information even if you get the worst of
it."

But Jawaharlal was not in this respect his father's
son. He disliked both slapping people's backs and punch-
ing their noses. Yet in his own quiet way he sized up
his surroundings and began to absorb whatever he
found that could be of use to him.

At first he was lonely and homesick. It was all a long
way from India—the little town on the hill, the steep
streets full of straw-hatted boys commuting between
classes, the tall trees and green playing fields, the
communal life, the emphasis on sport. "I was never an
exact fit," he said afterward. But he was not unpopular.
The masters liked him. One wrote: "You have every
reason to be proud of your son who is doing excel-
lently and making his mark in the school. Every
master who has anything to do with him, speaks in the
highest terms of his ability and his industry. He is a
thoroughly good fellow and ought to have a very
bright future before him."

The boys liked him too, vaguely. They just did not
remember him very well. The Indians were not con-
demned as a class, but taken on their merits. Young
Nehru was neither popular like an older contemporary
who happened to be very good at cricket nor unpopular

like a younger one who made the mistake of threatening what he would do to anyone who annoyed him if he ever stepped over the border of his father's state. "I was left a little to myself," Jawaharlal said. "I must confess," he wrote to his father during his second term, "I cannot mix properly with English boys. My tastes and inclinations are quite different."

It was true. At the time he was conducting a serious discussion with his father on the subject of his own marriage, and marriage was far enough from the minds of English sixteen-year-olds. Boys of his own age, he found, did not go much further than practical jokes and the politics of the games field. Jawaharlal was passionately interested in the world of real politics—much more so, at this time, than his father was. Even British politics interested him. In the winter of 1905 there was an important General Election in Britain, a Liberal government replacing the Conservatives after ten years. Young Nehru was the only boy in his class who seemed to have read the papers. He astonished the form master and the other boys by rattling off the names of the new cabinet.

British politics, or the war between Russia and Japan, or the Wright brothers' airplane were subjects he could sometimes talk about to sympathetic listeners. But his much more passionate interest in Indian politics had to stay locked up. Indian nationalism was stirring at last, especially in Bengal, and Jawaharlal, radical as all schoolboys tend to be, let off steam enthusiastically to his father in his letters. "I do not . . . approve of your politics," his father wrote back rather severely.

Motilal was not the man to welcome disturbances at home.

As soon as Jawaharlal could, which was as soon as his father would let him, after two years at Harrow, he went on up to the university at Cambridge. He was only seventeen, but he had outgrown school. Motilal urged him again to be "the most popular young fellow and the most distinguished graduate of Cambridge." Jawaharlal was not cut out for either distinction.

He liked Cambridge, and he liked his college, Trinity. There is peace in the quiet brick and stone quadrangles linking one into the other until you come out through gardens to the river's edge. It is a kind of peace that mixes very well with the restlessness of young men talking politics and ethics and putting the world to rights in their rooms after midnight. Jawaharlal liked walking the narrow streets of Cambridge, strolling by its river, swimming in its pools, taking a punt on lazy summer afternoons up to Grantchester to eat strawberries and cream under the apple trees. Chemistry, geology, and botany were his subjects of study, and he enjoyed his work. Best of all, he liked talking to his friends, because here he found friends with whom he could talk.

They discussed India and Indian nationalism endlessly in their upper-class English accents; most of them were destined for the Indian Civil Service, that steel frame of British rule. "We considered ourselves very sophisticated and talked of sex and morality in a superior way. We felt that we knew as much about the theory of the subject as anyone who was not a specialist

need know." Life was very, very pleasant in those
"three quiet years with little of disturbance in them,
moving slowly like the sluggish Cam."

Jawaharlal emerged from his education externally
an English gentleman, internally a fiery nationalist, at
least in theory, longing for a life of adventure and a
chance to play a brave part in Indian politics. "I have
become a queer mixture of the East and West," he said
once, "out of place everywhere, at home nowhere."

At a quick glance one would only have seen the West
in the rich man's son who came down from Cambridge
to London and read for the Bar without enthusiasm.
(He did not really want to be a lawyer, but the Indian
Civil Service would take him too far from home, and he
had been away from home long enough; these were the
only two practical options.) This young man had his
suits and his hats and his shoes made as expensively as
his father's. He wore high collars and wide silk cravats,
had about him an air of conscious aristocracy, and
carried a gold watch chain. He seemed quite in his
natural habitat when he went to the most exclusive
shops in London to order a court dress for Motilal. King
George V was visiting India to celebrate his coronation,
and the elder Nehru was one of the distinguished
gentlemen requested to attend the ceremonies. It meant
black velvet and ruffles, silver-buckled shoes, ceremonial
sword—the lot. It was expensive but worth it. (Ten
years later, father and son would both be in jail for
defying that same British raj.)

Jawaharlal and his father did not always agree. The

son was a haughty young man, as the father found out when he wrote to London to complain about the way money was melting away. He had meant Jawaharlal to live freely and generously, he didn't grudge a single rupee, but . . . He was caught, as successful self-made men so often are, between pride in giving his son everything he himself had missed and a jealous fear that money is a softening influence, that the youngsters of today don't understand what economy, industry, discipline are all about.

Jawaharlal (you can see his nostrils flaring) wrote back: "May I know if I am supposed to keep you informed of every penny I spend on a bus fare or a stamp? Either you trust me or you do not. If you do then surely no accounts are necessary? If you do not, then the accounts I send you are not to be relied on . . . I am not desirous of staying in England or anywhere else under these conditions."

Nothing could really disturb the relationship between father and son, and this brief tiff was soon forgotten in the excitement of Jawaharlal's homecoming. He was twenty-two and a barrister. He had been seven years away, with only two short holidays in India. Now he was coming home for good. Builders were set to work on Anand Bhawan to make sure that Jawaharlal, the only son, had the right kind of living space, and Motilal looked forward to working with his son in the law courts—a famous legal team, the Nehrus of Allahabad.

Mahatma Gandhi

And now it was August 1912, that distant golden age when money was money and the world was at peace, and the Nehru family were spending the hot-weather months at Mussoorie. Swaruprani had forgotten all her ailments and was in an ecstasy of excitement to welcome home her son. Only Krishna, the five-year-old, sulked—so she remembered later. She was a stormy child, and it did not seem fair that the beautiful mother who never had time in the midst of ill health and household cares to be "a proper mother" to her was obviously going to find time to be a proper mother to the grown-up son. Krishna was well aware, and it marked her growing-up, that her mother was always disappointed to have had a second daughter instead of a second son.

Her small heart sank when the tall young man rode up from the railway station looking so like the mother who welcomed him with shining eyes. Krishna was torn between longing to love and be loved, and determination not to become one of the worshipping crowd. "So this is the baby sister? She is quite a little lady now." Jawaharlal swung her up and put her down and she was affronted because he forgot her immediately. Something of this duality remained in their relationship forever after.

The Nehrus were a family of strong feelings and stormy crosscurrents, and in this it was much like the India that Jawaharlal came home to. Nothing much was seen on the surface, but the ground swell was working and soon the waves of India's nationalism would begin to rise.

We must turn now from the Nehrus to a man of whom it was said that he was the crest of that huge wave—Mohandas Gandhi. During the years of the First World War, while the wave gathered strength and Jawaharlal pottered idly at home, dreaming of great deeds but not yet seeing a way to them, the name of Gandhi began to be heard, at first faintly, then louder and louder. He was to be, for the Nehrus as for all India, their leader, their inspiration, and their saint.

Mohandas Gandhi was the youngest child of a respectable family from Western India. His father was an intelligent, brave, straightforward person, but no more so than thousands of other Indian men. His mother was deeply religious, but no more so than thousands of other Indian women. The child was not announced by angels, and behaved very much like

other boys. He was particularly quiet, shy, and unself-
confident. He found it difficult to learn the multiplica-
tion tables, and he smoked in secret, stealing the money
from the household servant to buy cigarettes.

At thirteen he was married to a bride of thirteen; this
was in the 1880's, before the government had raised the
age for marriage. "Two innocent children all unwit-
tingly hurled themselves into the ocean of life," he said
later. Of course they still lived with the parents and
Mohandas still went to school, but he domineered over
his young wife a little and expected her to ask his per-
mission every time she went out to play with the other
girls. He said that he had learned his first lesson in
passive resistance from the methods she used to get her
own way.

At the age of nineteen, small, ugly, and defenseless,
but with unexpected reserves of determination, Mohandas sailed off to England to study law. He was
brave enough to go in spite of the disapproval of many
in his community, but he was too frightened on board
the ship to emerge from his cabin; he did not dare tackle
the strange food and stranger eating implements in the
salon.

He was a slightly comic figure in London. He was
determined to wear European clothes, learn European
dancing, play a European violin, and speak with an
English accent, and he failed grotesquely on every
count. Yet people who met him did not find him easy to
forget. All the time he was growing up, but most
of his growth was internal. In between his law studies,

he found food and drink in the New Testament and the *Bhagavad-Gita*, a philosophical Hindu poem.

"Lay not up for yourselves treasures upon earth, where moth and rust do corrupt, and where thieves break through and steal: but lay up for yourselves treasures in heaven . . . for where your treasure is, there will your heart be also."

"When a man surrenders all desires that come to the heart and by the grace of God finds the joy of God, then his soul has indeed found peace."

He returned to India, but he was too shy to work as a lawyer. He broke down in his first speech and someone else had to finish it for him. His family must have wondered whether they were going to get their money's worth out of Mohandas or if he were going to be a failure all his life. They were no doubt relieved when in 1893 he was offered a job in South Africa. It was supposed to last a year, but in fact it was twenty-two years before he finally came back to his homeland, and by that time he was famous.

Gandhi had barely reached South Africa when something happened that was, he said later, the "most creative experience" in his life. He had occasion to travel by overnight train and had bought a first-class ticket and got into a first-class compartment. A white man looked in, wanted to enter, but refused to share the carriage with an Indian, so he called in the railway officials and Gandhi was told to travel in the luggage car. He would not submit to such obvious injustice and preferred to get out and sit all night shivering on the station platform, thinking. "It has always been a mystery to me," he once said, "how men can feel themselves honoured by the humiliation of their fellow beings."

Within a week he had called a meeting of Indians in South Africa to talk about racial injustice. This time he was not too shy to make his point. Gandhi's lifework had begun.

The Indians had first come into South Africa as laborers to work the tea and coffee plantations. They were hard-working and had large families and by this date there was a large Indian population, much of it prosperous and middle class. The South African whites were moved by the fear of being swamped by a tide of darker color which has been at the root of all their actions then and since. They tried to stifle and discourage the Indians, whom they referred to as "coolies." Laws were passed which deprived them of the vote, made them carry passes, taxed them heavily, and forbade them to own property. But there were by now 100,000 Indians, which is a lot of people to stifle. Moreover, the Indians had found a leader.

It was now that Gandhi discovered and developed a new political force which was later to be the key to India's struggle for independence. It has since been called "passive resistance," or "civil disobedience," but Gandhi's own word was stronger and truer. He called it *satyagraha*—"soul force." The man who has integrity and follows his conscience totally, without hatred or malice, whatever may happen to him, has a strength that is more than the strength of armies. To be faced

by people who will not obey and can\
is a terrifying thing for an army o\
They have to resort to violence without \
shames what is decent in man, so that they\
themselves up to artificial anger or ackno\
they are beaten. It only works, of course, in   _y
where there is fundamental regard for huma_ rights,
however confused people have become about them. As
Gandhi said, there is no *satyagraha* about the mouse
allowing itself to be torn to pieces by the cat.

At the height of the campaign in South Africa, thousands of Indians were in jail for peacefully breaking
laws they considered to be morally wrong—and as fast
as they came out of jail they broke the laws again and
went back in. At one time, fifty thousand were on
strike and five thousand in prison, and Gandhi himself
led a march of two thousand over a forbidden border,
courting arrest.

It was too much. The government gave in. General
Jan Christiaan Smuts and Gandhi met to negotiate and
the result was an agreement that Gandhi called a
Magna Carta for South African Indians. "It was my
fate," said General Smuts, "to be the antagonist of a
man for whom even then I had the highest respect
. . . He never forgot the human background of the
situation, never lost his temper or succumbed to hate,
and preserved his gentle humour in the most trying
situations. His manner and spirit even then as well as
later, contrasted markedly with the ruthless and brutal
forcefulness which is in vogue in our day."

In 1915, after twenty-two years in South Africa, Gandhi came back to be the soul and conscience of India in her struggle for independence.

It was in 1916, on February 8, the festival that heralds the coming of spring, and, the astrologers said, a suitable and fortunate day, that a marriage was arranged between Jawaharlal Nehru and a lovely, shy, seventeen-year-old, Kamala Kaul, daughter of a Kashmiri businessman from Delhi. Jawaharlal's little sister, Krishna, remembered peering from the verandah at a party in the Anand Bhawan drawing-room which she was too young to join, and seeing Kamala for the first time.

"Do you see that girl?" Bibi Amma said. "She's going to be your sister-in-law."

Krishna never forgot "the utter youthfulness and freshness that were Kamala's when she was seventeen," and in later years the whole family recalled sadly that the most attractive thing about her then was her radiant good health. She was in every way a good match for Jawaharlal. Her English was not very good, however, so she had lessons from the English governess. Motilal adored her at once. Nan, who was the same age, was more than a little jealous. We do not know what Swaruprani's reactions were, but it seems unlikely that she found it easy to accept any girl as good enough for her son.

The wedding was as splendid as might have been expected. For months beforehand, or so it seemed,

Anand Bhawan was full of clerks making arrangements, giving and taking orders, consulting about invitations. Jewelers and tailors and shopkeepers of every sort scuttled in and out. A week before the event a special decorated train took the Allahabad contingent to Delhi, where they were joined by relations from all over India in a village of tents erected for the occasion. The fun went on for weeks before the party broke up, and then the Nehrus, with the new bride among them, went north to Kashmir, to escape the hot weather.

They came back to Allahabad later in the year and life went on as usual. Marriage no doubt made a good deal of difference to Kamala, but at first it made very little difference to Jawaharlal. He still lived at home in precisely the same fashion as before. At this time his life was in the doldrums. The law bored him. Allahabad was provincial. His marriage was not particularly exciting —nor had he expected it to be; Indian marriages grow slowly to maturity.

The first excitement perhaps which he fully shared with his young wife was the birth of a daughter. On the nineteenth of November 1917, five days after Jawaharlal's own twenty-eighth birthday, Indira Pryadarshini Nehru arrived, with a wealth of black hair, dark eyes, and two solemn straight black eyebrows. Mrs. Sarojini Naidu, the poetess, sent congratulations—"Love to all and a kiss to the new Soul of India"—but the letter was a month late because of Mrs. Naidu's involvement in political affairs.

The new Soul of India was very much the soul of

Anand Bhawan—not quite so much as if she had been a boy, perhaps, but enough for any baby, from adoring grandparents, parents, and aunts, to all the rest of that large household. "I am always thinking of Indira," Motilal wrote once when he was away from home. "The very thought of a personification of innocence is soothing." And he ordered her a suitable baby carriage from Calcutta.

Let her have as much attention as she can while she can. The iron hand of public affairs would soon descend and push her aside into as insecure and ignored a growing-up as ever a child had. Kamala did not recover quickly from her daughter's birth, and it was not very long afterward that she first began to show signs of the tuberculosis that dogged her the rest of her life.

Indira (Indu, they called her at home) was born, as her father often reminded her later, in the very month of the Russian Revolution, and her whole early life was colored, not like that of other children with the trivial events of home life, but with the struggles of a country trying to attain nationhood.

Jawaharlal as a little boy had learned his nationalism from old stories of the Mutiny, long past, while he himself lived in security. Indira's earliest years shook with tales of tragedy here and now. Anglo-Indian violence to Jawaharlal meant bouncing cousins with loud voices telling stories of quarrels in railway carriages. To Indira it meant tales like that of the massacre of Jallianwala Bagh, which happened when she was a baby.

In 1919, India was restless as the whole world was restless with the ending of the First World War. Nationalism was very much in the air. In Europe nationhood was being given to small peoples who claimed it: Estonians, Czechs, Poles. Millions of Indians stirred and stretched under the British hand.

The troubles of March 1919 were triggered by the Rowlatt Acts. The British called them a necessary safeguard: in uncertain times you must be able to enforce law and order, harshly if necessary. Indian nationalists saw only that this kind of special power (arrest without warning, imprisonment without trial) was degrading and anti-democratic. Never mind that in fact the acts were never used; they were there, and that was enough.

Gandhi called for a *hartal* in protest. A *hartal* is something more than a general strike, it is a complete stoppage of all activity for one day or longer. Gandhi saw it as pure *satyagraha:* a whole nation shows that it is too hurt and upset to do anything but go into mourning behind closed doors, a gesture of great dignity. But India was in an excitable mood, easily brought to boiling point. *Hartal* leaves people with nothing to do but talk about their wrongs.

The riots simmered in the cities of the north. There were ugly incidents, strong police action, murders, beatings, even firing on crowds. Everyone was on edge and the British thought back, as they always did in explosive situations, to the massacres of the Mutiny.

Amritsar, a city of the Sikhs, was particularly restive. Mobs gathered, there was burning and looting. A white woman was severely beaten and left for dead in a narrow lane (and incidentally rescued by an Indian). In this menacing situation, and in the teeth of an order forbidding all meetings, a huge mass meeting gathered in the Jallianwala Bagh, a piece of waste ground, once a garden, in the center of the city. It was a mixed meeting, men predominating, but there were some women and a good many children; the Bagh was a sort of unofficial children's playground for the quarter. Meetings had been forbidden, but many of those attending had come from villages on the outskirts and probably did not know of the prohibition; those who did know did not care. It was an unarmed meeting as far as guns went, though there were probably plenty of sticks about.

Jallianwala Bagh has very few exits—a few tiny lanes, mere passages, into the surrounding streets. There was also at one side a wall about five feet high. For the rest, the space was surrounded by buildings.

The British officer in charge of the district, General Reginald E. H. Dyer, wanted to deal one swift blow to impose quiet on Amritsar. As long as the mob seethed in narrow alleys he could do very little, but here they had delivered themselves into his hands. He had few soldiers at his disposal but he struck quickly. Ninety men, fifty with rifles, marched into the Jallianwala Bagh while the crowd listened to the speakers. The fifty men with rifles lined up on slightly higher ground, from which they overlooked the whole park.

There was no warning, no firing in the air, no time for parley, and, of course, no way out. The fifty soldiers fired on the crowd until they ran out of ammunition.

The crowd broke into waves of screaming panic, beating on the walls and doorways, recoiling and beating again, trampling one another underfoot. After fifteen minutes the military marched out again, leaving fifteen hundred casualties. Most of them stayed all night where they fell, because a curfew had been imposed and their friends could not come to carry them away. The dogs and the vultures had a busy time before morning.

A great deal of ink has been used up in attempts to get to the bottom of this horrible occurrence. Dyer was not a hired murderer. He was a stolid soldier, a third-generation Anglo-Indian, born in Simla and for thirty-one years in the Indian army, and was popular with his men, whose languages he spoke fluently. Nor did his Indian soldiers feel that he was giving them an unthinkable order; they fired as he told them, coolly and regularly.

Dyer may have been arrogant, even slightly unbalanced. He may not have realized quite how difficult it would be for the crowd to disperse. He may have had real grounds for fears about the safety of Amritsar unless quick, sharp action were taken.

The fact remained that a decision had been taken with regard to an Indian crowd which could never conceivably have been taken with regard to a European crowd in the same circumstances. Whether it was tragedy or murder, the whole of India saw how little their lives counted in the political thinking of their masters.

The massacre was not the end of it. For a time the Punjab became a police state, with floggings and harsh punishments, the most bitterly resented of which was the "crawling order" which made Indians crawl on hands and knees through the lane where the white woman had been nearly beaten to death. "We'll show them who's master" was the motto, and the Punjab was a lot quieter for the next few months than most other states in India. But once rulers have to resort to such measures, their ultimate loss of power is already certain. It would take twenty-seven years, but Jallianwala Bagh made it inevitable. It was also inevitable that people like Jawaharlal Nehru, however Westernized outwardly, now knew where their sympathies and their work lay.

FIVE

The Fight Begins

Childhood, for most of us, is an endless time measured by birthdays, by holidays, by the first day of school, by the arrival of a new baby or the death of a pet. These events, important only inside the family, are the marked days.

It was not like that for Indira Gandhi. "I don't remember ever playing," she has said. Her childhood was measured by political activities, by the police tramping in and out, by her relations going to prison. In all of this, even as a mere baby, she took part. "I went everywhere, especially when the All-India Congress Committee was meeting. But the most important meetings were held on our lawn. So there was no question of having to go out to attend them."

It was hardly the kind of upbringing that Dr. Benjamin Spock would recommend. She was only lucky that, in her formative years, the struggle for freedom

which was in the air she breathed was on the whole a
noble struggle nobly conducted. "We had a sense of
freedom and a pride in that freedom," wrote Jawaharlal
in his autobiography. "We said what we felt and
shouted it out from the housetops. What did we care
for the consequences? Prison? We looked forward
to it."

And he wrote to his daughter when she was old
enough to understand: "How shall we bear ourselves in
this great movement? What part shall we play in it? I
cannot say what part will fall to our lot; but, whatever
it may be, let us remember that we can do nothing
which may bring discredit to our cause or dishonour to
our people. If we are to be India's soldiers we have
India's honour in our keeping, and that honour is a
sacred trust. Often we may be in doubt what to do. It is
no easy matter to decide what is right and what is not.
One little test I shall ask you to apply whenever you
are in any doubt. It may help you. Never do anything in secret or anything that you wish to hide. For
the desire to hide anything means that you are afraid,
and fear is a bad thing and unworthy of you . . .
And if you do so, my dear, you will grow up a child
of the light, unafraid and serene and unruffled, whatever may happen."

In her very early years, though, there was much
that was natural to childhood, and a fortunate childhood at that. Anand Bhawan was a lovely place for a
child to explore. The stables were full of horses, the
gardens of fruit and flowers and the shade of the huge

peepul tree with the stone statue in its branches. There
were delicious mornings spent sitting on the lawn eating
mangoes. And on hot days, there was the delightful
summerhouse, cool with the sound of running water
and the scent of flowers, where a statue of Shiva stood
on a pile of stones with a fountain playing from his
head. There were summer holidays with her parents in
the hills, and when they returned in the autumn there
was the Diwali festival, and after that her birthday.
Diwali celebrates Rama's return from exile, and it is a
festival of lights. There are sweets and presents too, but
the glory of the feast comes at twilight, when every
house is lit up. Anand Bhawan, with hundreds of tiny
oil lamps on every cornice and windowsill, became an
enchanted palace.

But the old order was already changing as father and
grandfather became more deeply committed to politics.
Jawaharlal plunged first, with all the pent-up emotion
of a man who is nearly thirty before he discovers the
real direction of his life. "I was simply bowled over by
Gandhi, straight off."

Motilal at first was doubtful, but when he joined his
son, he did so with the full force of his exuberant
personality.

Then came the great change at Anand Bhawan as
Gandhi called on people to reject foreign goods and
buy instead the Indian commodity. Suddenly and
dramatically, Motilal and Jawaharlal changed their
pinstripes and silk ties for *khadi*, coarse white homespun. Shining top hats were stowed away in favor of the

white Gandhi cap. Motilal looked superb as ever, but no
longer like an English earl, more like a Roman emperor.
His enthusiasm for clearing foreign stuff out of Anand
Bhawan, for sitting on the floor and eating simple rice
and vegetables instead of "breakfast, lunch, and dinner
à l'Anglaise" for a while knew no bounds. Many of the
servants, and the carriages and horses and motorcars,
disappeared. There were limits, however: when Jawaharlal took to going on political errands around the
town in a creaking bullcart, Motilal felt that this was
going too far. "If you want to come up to the house,
leave that monstrosity at the gate," he bawled at his
son from the verandah on one occasion when he was
entertaining friends.

When Nan married Ranjit Pandit in 1921, she did
not suffer for the new ideas. Although she was married
in a homespun sari as a gesture to the movement, her
trousseau included one hundred and one others, glowing
heaps of silk and finest cotton, with all the blouses and
slippers and jewels to go with them. Motilal gave his
daughter both an automobile and a riding horse.

The changes at Anand Bhawan fell heavily on the
women, all the same; or at least they did so at first. One
gets the impression that Motilal's enthusiasm waned
and that after a while old habits were allowed to creep
back. Krishna, fourteen years old now, who had not long
since escaped from governesses to a real school, which
she loved, was summarily removed because it was an
English school. The announcement went forth that
only *khadi* would be worn, and here perhaps Swaru-

prani suffered most. In those early days, *khadi* was coarse and heavy; to women accustomed to fine things it was like wearing tarpaulin, and Swaruprani tottered under the weight. But Kamala took to the new ways with a quiet determination that no one had suspected of her. In fact, to some extent it was owing to her that many of the changes were made.

"When my father wanted to join Gandhiji and to change the whole way of life, to change our luxurious living, to give up his practice, the whole family was against it," said Indira in later years. "It was only my mother's courageous and persistent support and encouragement which enabled him to take this big step which made such a difference not only to our family but to the history of modern India."

More was to follow. Motilal and Jawaharlal were both arrested for the first time that year. The occasion was partly comic, for the Nehrus were much too important for any police officer to enjoy the job. The unfortunate man shifted from foot to foot and could hardly produce his search warrant. When at last he did so, Motilal told him cheerfully to go ahead and search by all means but it would take six months to do justice to the house. The policeman wilted further and had to be encouraged to the point at which he could explain that there was also a warrant for arrest.

Indu saw her father and grandfather driven off to jail. She saw her mother and her grandmother hold their heads high, at least until the car had disappeared. For the first of many times she felt, however dimly,

the lonely confusion of a household from which the
heads of the house had gone and which, moreover, was
now subject to police raids. The Nehrus refused to
recognize the power of the British court and so would
not pay the fines imposed on them. The police came
more than once and took away carpets and furniture in
payment. Indu, who had inherited the family temper,
stamped her feet and stormed at them. To the men in
prison this was light relief; they laughed at the stories
of the four-year-old, knee-high to a police constable,
obstructing the course of justice with furious tears. But
to a child it was her security, her world, which was
vanishing, carted out of the door by uniformed ene-
mies. And she was right to protest—nothing could ever
be the same again.

She was quiet enough at her grandfather's trial. Was
it, perhaps, that her father and grandfather felt the
third generation's political education could not begin
soon enough? Solemn and uncomprehending, she sat
on Motilal's knee all through the proceedings. The
courtroom had been improvised inside the jail, and this
was her first acquaintance with the high brick walls,
the heavy doors and bolts and bunches of jangling keys
which were to be woven into the rest of her childhood.

That year the annual meeting of the Indian National Congress was held at Ahmedebad. (Congress had
been organized under British auspices as a political talking shop without power for the Indians, but it now
became the focus of the struggle for freedom, and since
independence it is still the main political party of

India.) Gandhi was settled at Ahmedebad, which is several hundred miles west of Allahabad, and he asked the Nehru women to attend the Congress and to stay the two weeks in his *ashram*.

They all—Swaruprani, Kamala, Krishna, and Indira —had their first taste of traveling third-class on the railway, and that, in India, is quite an experience. "One never thinks of travelling in any other carriage than first-class," an English lady had said. So far, the Nehrus had never thought of it either. Traveling first-class was the only way to have a little privacy, a little comfort. Each first-class compartment had another one opening from it, where one's servants traveled with the luggage, the cool drinks, the portable stove for making tea, and anything else that might be needed during the journey.

"Third-class passengers are treated like sheep and their comforts are sheep's comforts," Gandhi bluntly said after he had experienced this other way of traveling. He went on to describe vividly the overcrowding, the pushing, the noise, the betel chewing, the spitting and smoking and swearing, which made "third-class travelling a trial for a passenger of cleanly ways."

It must have been a great trial for Swaruprani. The children did not mind, and as for the delicate Kamala— people were beginning to see a certain light in Kamala's eye which they had not noticed before, as though perhaps she positively preferred things to be tough.

Then, at Gandhi's *ashram* beside the river, they had their first experience of his kind of simple living, com-

pared with which the reforms at Anand Bhawan were
make-believe. They slept in communal dormitories on
the floor and were roused at four in the cold morning
for prayers. The food was plain and almost completely
tasteless—Krishna dreamed hungrily of a square meal.
They had to do their own washing, and those saris
were like sodden blankets in the water. They were glad
to get home again, even to the empty rooms of Anand
Bhawan.

On this first occasion, Indira was without a father
and Kamala without a husband for thirteen months,
except for a few days in the middle. The Nehrus' short
time out of prison coincided, as it happened, with
Gandhi's going into it, and Jawaharlal used his brief
freedom to go to Ahmedebad and see his leader tried for
preaching sedition.

"I am here," Gandhi announced to the crowded
courtroom, "to invite and cheerfully submit to the
highest penalty that can be inflicted upon me for what
in law is a deliberate crime and what appears to me to be
the highest duty of a citizen."

It was in all ways a curious trial. As the judge
pronounced the sentence of six years (Gandhi served
only two of them), he bowed courteously to his prisoner. "The law is no respecter of persons," the judge
said. "Nevertheless it will be impossible to ignore the
fact that you are in a different category from any
person I have ever tried or am likely to have to try. It
would be impossible to ignore the fact that, in the eyes
of millions of your countrymen, you are a great

patriot and a great leader. Even those who differ from
you in politics look upon you as a man of high ideals
and of noble and even saintly life."

No doubt Indira, four and a half years old and now
well able to understand these things in her own fashion,
heard all about Gandhi's trial. Jawaharlal, stirred easily
and deeply by noble words and noble motives, must
have told the story most movingly. Perhaps it was under
this influence that Indira, as she remembers, used to
collect her dolls and preach to them, urging them too
to go to prison for freedom's sake. Sometimes she found
a more responsive audience and made fiery political
speeches to the servants from the top of a table.

Then father was taken away once more, and the
family settled down, on the outside of the walls, to a
routine of prison letters and prison visits as he settled
down to his own routine inside the walls. There was no
holiday in the hills that year, and the hot months in
Allahabad are really hot. The child was not well.
Jawaharlal was worried to see her so pale and weak
when Kamala brought her to the prison on a visit. But
it did not do to worry too much over things one could
do nothing about.

Prison, which has rotted the fibers of many men
apparently stronger than Jawaharlal Nehru, did him,
in the long run, nothing but good. He was a reader and
here was time to read. He was a thinker and here was
time to think. His vision of India, his own idealistic
brand of socialism, what he felt his country needed and
what must be done, developed and matured during the

time he spent in jail. Each release (altogether he spent
nine years in prison, the last three in detention, with
no idea when he would get out) found him a more
composed, a more disciplined, a more experienced man.

In the first thirteen months Nehru set his own pattern
of passing the days profitably—reading, writing, and
spinning cotton on his *charkha*. The spinning wheel was
Gandhi's symbol of self-help for the poor of India. By
it he hoped to establish a home industry which was to
lift them out of their poverty, and all his followers
were urged to spend some time each day in spinning.
Jawaharlal in prison worked hard; it was relatively
simple to get some kind of yarn but difficult to get it
fine and even. Indira too had a little spinning wheel that
her grandfather had got for her. Father and she ex-
changed messages and hanks of yarn between Anand
Bhawan and Lucknow jail.

After this first vigorous campaign for freedom, India
over the next few years fell into a mood of disillusion-
ment. Moslems and Hindus turned to quarreling among
themselves instead of working together in a cause
greater than either of them. Things did not go well at
Anand Bhawan either. For a while everybody seemed
to have lost direction, and Motilal and his son un-
happily drifted apart. At one moment Gandhi, loved
and trusted by both, had to step in and explain them
to each other. The trouble on this occasion was over
Indira's schooling. She was seven, and Motilal was in
favor of her going to school in Allahabad, where she
would find companions of her own age. But it was a

school run by three British ladies, and to Jawaharlal, always more extreme than his father, this was too much like supporting the raj.

This argument was only one of many. Underlying the strain was Jawaharlal's hatred of being still dependent on his father. He had given up all legal work to devote himself to politics, and politics was unpaid. Motilal pointed out that it was foolish to be scrupulous, since he could earn in a week enough for his son's family to live on for a year—which was perfectly true but cannot have been easy to swallow.

And, too, Kamala was not well. But at least the slackness in political affairs meant that Jawaharlal had more time for his family. They drew closer together. He was just beginning to understand that his young wife (she was only twenty-five) had not had an easy time of it since they were married and that he, in particular, had given her very little companionship.

The sadness of that November must have done much to draw them together. It was Indira's seventh birthday, and she had the most delightful present (although it arrived two days late) that any child could hope for. A brother for her, a son for Jawaharlal and Kamala, a grandson for Motilal and Swaruprani! The rejoicing did not last long, however, for the baby died within a week. Indu was the only child again, and remained so. History had repeated itself. No doubt her father told her, to comfort her a little, that he himself had had a baby brother on his sixteenth birthday, who had died soon afterward. The Nehrus seemed to be fated in their sons.

But at least there was a baby in the family; Aunt Nan
had had a daughter, who by now was sitting up and
cutting her teeth, but a girl cousin, however charming,
is not to be compared with having a brother all to
oneself.

The next birthday was not much more cheerful,
because by then Kamala was in the hospital. Her bouts
of ill health had been diagnosed as tuberculosis, and she
had to spend a whole winter in the hospital in Lucknow.
Then the following year a Swiss sanatorium was rec-
ommended, so they all went to Europe, and Indira's
ninth birthday was spent in very different surroundings, at the International School in Geneva. Even there,
politics took first place to family affairs; her grandfather had to write to apologize that he had been too
busy to send a birthday present.

He was not only busy with politics. He was building
a new house, a new Anand Bhawan, in the garden of
the old one—a small, economical, compact house more
fitting to followers of Gandhi. By the time it was finished, it was clearly Motilal's house, with great ele-
gance and charm, but neither small nor economical.
It was, however, smaller than the old house, which was
given over to the Congress Party and renamed "Swaraj
Bhawan," "Freedom House."

And so on a curious switchback of riches and poverty, possessions and deprivations, Indira proceeded
through her childhood, a very small dinghy in the
crosscurrents of family and national affairs, having a
fearfully rough ride in the waves which the big boats

hardly noticed. She was eleven, for instance, when her father came home cut and bruised from his first experience of a police *lathi* charge. He was leading a demonstration when it was broken up by mounted police wielding their six-foot, metal-tipped poles. Jawaharlal was introspective enough, even in those circumstances, to be more interested in his own reactions than in his injuries.

"We held our ground, and, as we appeared to be unyielding, the horses had to pull up at the last moment and reared up on their hind legs with their front hoofs quivering in the air over our heads. And then began a beating of us, and battering with *lathis* and long batons both by the mounted and the foot police. It was a tremendous hammering, and the clearness of vision that I had had the evening before left me. All I knew was that I had to stay where I was, and must not yield or go back. I felt half blinded with the blows, and sometimes a dull anger seized me, and a desire to hit out. I thought how easy it would be to pull down the police officer in front of me from his horse and to mount up myself, but long training and discipline held and I did not raise a hand, except to protect my face from a blow."

Her father beaten up by the police! And yet two weeks later the whole family were proudly scattering flower petals from a balcony in Calcutta as Motilal went past, the newly elected president of Congress. It was a superb pageant of welcome. He rode in a carriage drawn by thirty-four white horses, ridden by postilions in red and green uniforms, the Congress colors, clearing the crowds with flourished whips. There was a salute of 101 rockets, and so many flowers were thrown into the carriage that before the end of the ride Motilal, acutely embarrassed, could hardly see over the top.

There was an even prouder moment to come. The following year Jawaharlal was elected president, and they had the excitement of seeing the famous father hand over the office to his famous son. Swaruprani was almost beside herself with pride and joy. Congress was in Lahore that year, and Jawaharlal rode in like a king on a white horse, supported by troops of Congress volunteers in neat khaki uniforms with yellow facings, with the band playing "The Wearing o' the Green," a protest song borrowed from the Irish rebellions. The streets were gay with bunting, and bystanders swarmed in windows, on roofs, even in the branches of trees, throwing down flowers on their hero. For many in India Jawaharlal had become the mythical Young Hero, the Shining Knight, the Sword-in-Hand Deliverer who fights the Beast.

"In bravery he is not to be surpassed. Who can excel him in the love of the country?" Gandhi wrote of him. " 'He is rash and impetuous,' say some. This quality is an additional qualification at the present moment. And if he has the dash and rashness of a warrior, he has also the prudence of a statesman. He is undoubtedly an extremist, thinking far ahead of his surroundings. But he is humble enough not to force the pace to the breaking point. He is pure as crystal, he is truthful beyond suspicion. He is a knight *sans peur and sans reproche*. The nation is safe in his hands."

Who can doubt that this fairy-tale atmosphere was eagerly absorbed by the quiet little girl whom nobody particularly noticed but who was always there? She was just twelve, the political niceties must have been out of her grasp, but not the vivid picture of the two generations ahead of her. How would she fulfill the challenge of being the third generation?

Year of Unrest

And so, with Jawaharlal Nehru as president of Congress, began 1930, the year of unrest which was to show the world that Gandhi's revolutionary ideas could, in certain circumstances, work. The circumstances are, of course, a ruling power that is not, or cannot afford to be, too ruthless, that has one eye on world public opinion.

On January 26, 1930, Gandhi called for an "Independence Day" when people would swear that it was "a crime against man and God to submit to British rule." We may imagine that no one took the oath with more fervor than Indu and her young Pandit cousins, with shining eyes and shrill voices, waving Congress flags bigger than themselves. The only part of the movement they did not appreciate was having to wear *khadi* and those ugly caps when other girls had pretty things, silks and ribbons. Indira complained directly to Gandhi on at least one occasion, and he took the trouble to explain the matter seriously and patiently, exactly as he would have explained to a beggar or a king. Gandhi was no respecter of persons, which means that he respected all persons.

"He gave his whole attention—I mean you felt that to him it was just as much of a problem as it was to you, and even if you didn't agree with him you came back satisfied that the thing had been thrashed out," Indira much later said of him. It was the reason for his success as a leader; he belonged completely to those he led.

"Ordinary men and women are not usually heroic. They think of their bread and butter, of their children, of their household worries and the like. But a time comes when a whole people becomes full of faith for a great cause, and then even simple, ordinary men and women become heroes, and history becomes stirring and epoch-making," Jawaharlal Nehru wrote. "Great leaders have something in them which inspires a whole people and makes them do great deeds."

Such a leader was the elderly Mahatma, small-statured, toothless (he rarely wore his false teeth, because the peasants could not afford them), steel-spectacled, wearing only the peasants' white loincloth and shawl. There have been many strange crusades but none stranger, and as it turned out none more inspired, than the one which Gandhi started in March 1930. He feared the outbreak of violence, always endemic in an excitable people under a hot sun, and since Indepen-

dence Day he had been thinking while India waited for
his word. What was the right method by which to offer
at once the most peaceful and the most powerful non-
cooperation? The answer was as brilliant as, at first, it
seemed comically insufficient.

He chose the salt tax, a tax which personally involved every single one of India's millions. The actual
tax on each family was small but not negligible to the
poor; he worked out that the average peasant paid three
days' earnings to the government each year by this
tax. The ignorant could not easily be interested by
high-flown theories of freedom, but this announcement
caught their imaginations. The method by which
Gandhi proposed to break the law was equally inspired.
He would walk with his chosen followers from his
ashram to the sea, a distance of 240 miles, and there
pick up salt left by the waves. And when he did so, all
over India others would do the same, picking up salt
if they lived by the sea, or, if they lived inland, boiling
their own salt illegally in public places. When they
were arrested, they would accept their punishment and
go peacefully to prison.

As one of Gandhi's biographers has said, this gesture
required "imagination, dignity, and the sense of show-
manship of a great artist." In the twenty-four days of
the march, there was time for the whole of India to look
up and hold its breath. And they saw a leader who was
clothed like them and who traveled like them, with a
stick and a pair of sandals along the dusty roads.

By the time Gandhi reached the sea, the crowd with

him numbered thousands, including newsmen from all over the world. He ceremoniously picked up a handful of unusable sandy salt, and on the same day in five thousand other places all over India the law was broken by people boiling their own salt. (Ironically, most of them first had to buy government salt in order to have something to boil, but the point was made.)

The salt water boiling in illegal pans did not bubble more fiercely than India that summer. Thousands were arrested, perhaps as many as a hundred thousand. The prisons were crowded. Jawaharlal was one of the first; as president of Congress, he was in a vulnerable position. He was sentenced to six months to be served in Naini prison, just across the river from Allahabad, so near that you could see it from the flat roof of Anand Bhawan, where the Congress flag flew defiantly from its staff.

It was much less easy to be in prison that summer than it had been before. After the first acceptance of arrest, the trial, the sentence, all of which made one feel that this was really serving freedom's cause, there was nothing but the deflating monotony of prison life. There were not even hardships to keep up one's self-esteem, for "A" prisoners were treated almost with tenderness. There was the heat, of course, and the dust and the flies, but those were things which poor people had to accept every year, without being in prison.

"The thought that I was having a relatively easy time in prison, at a time when others were facing danger and suffering outside, began to oppress me. I longed to go out, and as I could not do that, I made my life in prison a hard one, full of work." He also asked his family not to send in ice and fruit, as these were luxuries that others could not afford. With the thermometer working up into the hundreds, this in its small way was a heroic request.

Jawaharlal was soon joined by his brother-in-law, Ranjit Pandit, and his father. Motilal was an elderly man now, much troubled by asthma. The authorities offered to build another verandah to the barrack to make him more comfortable. They also asked the two Nehrus what food they would need. Motilal courteously assured the superintendent that he had long been accustomed to the simplest fare and then began to recite his minimum needs while the poor man's mouth dropped open.

"Nonsense, Father," said Jawaharlal sharply, "this is a prison, not a hotel."

But he nursed his father, that hot summer in jail, with a devotion which brought the two closer together than ever. They had never, in any case, done more than disagree on the surface because they loved one another too well. After a few weeks Motilal was released on grounds of health, and Jawaharlal was left to his self-imposed routine of reading, spinning and weaving, getting up very early to escape the heat and make the best use of daylight.

The most exciting aspect of the great nonviolent campaign which rolled like a wave across the country that summer was the release of the women into political work as their menfolk were bundled off to jail.

Gandhi's object was not just to get rid of foreign rule. He wanted India to grow a new soul to meet the challenge, and one of his objectives was precisely this: to rescue the women from the restrictions of *purdah*, as he wanted to rescue the sweeper class, the "untouchables" (he renamed them *harijans*, "children of God"), and as he wanted to bridge the gap between Hindus and Moslems. Devout Hindu though he was, he was above the shackles of superstition.

In the Nehru family, because they were Kashmiris and because they were Westernized, the women had always had a good deal of freedom, and they moved now with a will into the front line. They organized processions, they addressed meetings, they picketed shops to prevent foreign goods being sold. Even Swaruprani, elderly and aristocratic as she was, joined the fight, though she could not go the whole way with her daughters and daughters-in-law. Particularly she drew the line at their wearing trousers for front-line work, as she had already protested in vain when they cut their hair short.

Kamala's real character began to show now. Switzerland's healing effects had long worn off, and she was often ill. Moreover, she missed her husband badly, but out of the fragile body shone forth the soul of a dedicated soldier. "How I wish I were arrested before you come out!" she wrote to Jawaharlal.

She was up at five in the morning to drill her body of
women volunteers and by eight o'clock was on picket
duty outside the shops that sold foreign goods. In
blazing heat, later in the cold, she never flagged or
grumbled but sat patiently in demonstrations for hours
in all weathers.

Now that they were apart, she grew to equality in
her husband's eyes, and he heard with delight of
her exploits and realized, as he had never realized before, what a companion his wife could be. "Never can
I forget the thrill that came to us in Naini prison when
news of this reached us, the enormous pride in the
women of India that filled us. We could hardly talk
about all this among ourselves, for our hearts were full
and our eyes were dim with tears. . . . In this up-
heaval Kamala had played a brave and notable part,
and on her inexperienced shoulders fell the task of or-
ganizing our work in the city of Allahabad when every
known worker was in prison. She made up for that in-
experience by her fire and energy and, within a few
months, she became the pride of Allahabad."

Like many others, she could never again be labeled
"only a woman." And how Indira longed not to be
labeled "only a child"! At the height of the disturbances
there was room in the movement for the children too.
This twelve-year-old, uniformed in *khadi* tunic and
trousers, Gandhi cap rakishly on her dark head, that
autumn was leading the children's brigade, the
"Monkey Army." "I suggest the wearing of a tail by
every member of it," wrote grandfather from jail, "the

length of which should be in proportion to the rank of
the wearer."

To the children it was no matter for smiling. They
flung themselves into the fight with all the enthusiasm
of their elders, and probably with much less restraint.
They were up just as early, drilling in the dark mornings. They did their stint of spinning. They helped to
picket shops. They delivered messages, they sewed
Congress flags in red and green and hung them im-
pudently in public places. Sometimes there were
more serious occasions. As the police force grew more
strained and angry, the *lathi* charges were more violent. Sometimes mobs were dispersed by shooting, and
at times the injured were left on the ground where they
fell, because people dared not come to their help.

"In those days," Indira later said, "when there was
firing, even though people were severely injured, no
doctor could come and treat them. The doctor could
only come when it was dark, when nobody could see
that he was coming and report him to the Government.
So, once when such firing took place in a village not far
from our home, we had to go ourselves to bring these
wounded and bleeding young boys, most of them
between the ages of 14 and 17, and we opened part of
our own home as a hospital ward. This was my intro-
duction to service because I was only 12 or 13 at the
time. But since we could not get anyone else, my
friends and I had to be the nurses for those very
seriously wounded people."

In October, Jawaharlal wrote to his sister: "If father

has finished with Garibaldi (the first volume about the
defence of the Roman Republic) send it to Indu . . . I
should like her to read it soon as I want to write to her
on the subject."

This was a book with the Harrow crest on it. Jawaharlal had been given it as a prize in his last term at
school, and at seventeen its stirring story of Italy's
great liberator had inspired his dreams of one day
freeing India from foreign rule. It was time for Indira
to share the dream. She had loved the story of Joan of
Arc when she was little; Garibaldi's story too has a
woman heroine, the lovely and high-spirited Anita, his
wife, who lived and fought at his side for ten years and
died in his arms on the battlefield. Here was a heroine
for a captain in the Monkey Army, tired of carrying
messages and thirsting for glory!

"Slipping away unnoticed from among her drunken
guards, she plunged into the tropical forest on a high-
spirited horse which she had obtained from a peasant,
crossed sixty miles of the most dangerous deserts in
America, alone, without food, swimming great rivers in
flood by holding on to her horse, riding through hostile
guards at the passes of the hills and the fords of the
streams, who took the wild Amazon for an apparition
and ran away in panic."

As the year ended, Indu needed something to lift
her spirits. Grandfather was ill. He had been ill for
some months, had been released from jail because of ill
health, and although she did not know that he was
dying, the approach of death settled like a cloud on the

house. It was reflected in the faces of people who came to see him, however hard they tried not to show it.

Then, on the first day of January 1931, Kamala was arrested and sentenced, and Indu, as best she could, had to face the prospect of the next six months without either parent. In fact, however, it was not even one month. Kamala, Ranjit, and Jawaharlal were all released because Motilal's death was near.

He died in February 1931. For all of them it was as though a strong tree which had sheltered and supported them had suddenly been axed. Jawaharlal in particular had the heart knocked out of him. In his autobiography he wrote: "As evening fell on the river bank on that winter day, the great flames leapt up and consumed that body which had meant so much to us who were close to him as well as the millions in India. Gandhiji said a few moving words to the multitude, and then all of us crept silently home. The stars were out and shining brightly when we returned, lonely and desolate."

Anand Bhawan echoed hollowly to their footsteps. It was, after all, only a shell.

The House of Peace

It was not all turbulence and sadness. After Motilal's death there followed a lovely interlude, all too short, which was as happy as anything that happened to Jawaharlal and his family. A truce between the British government and the Congress had resulted in a lull in political affairs, so Jawaharlal took Kamala and Indira on a holiday to Ceylon, which became two months of the purest pleasure.

First there was the relief from all the stresses of the past months. After nearly a year in prison, there was the joy of simply being free and seeing a distant horizon. Jawaharlal could not have enough of it, as their ship sailed quietly through the intense blue of the Arabian Sea toward a dim coastline.

It was their first tropical visit, and Ceylon is a beautiful country. Everything, moreover, was intensified by its comparison with prison walls. "I love to think of the cool tropical jungle," Jawaharlal wrote (a few months later, and back behind bricks again) "with its abundant life, looking at you with a thousand eyes; and of the graceful areca tree, slender and straight and true; and the innumerable coconuts, and the palm-fringed seashore where the emerald green of the island meets the blue of the sea and the sky; and the sea-water glistens and plays on the surf, and the wind rustles through the palm-leaves . . ."

A Technicolor paradise, too good to be true. But so it was—much too good to be true. Every moment was sharp with pleasure, because it was all inevitably going to end so soon. Best of all, there was Jawaharlal's relationship with Kamala. "We seemed to have discovered each other anew. All the past years that we had passed together had been but a preparation for this new and more intimate relationship. We came back all too soon and work claimed me and, later, prison. There was to be no more holidaying, no working together, except for a brief while . . . ."

Indira, that lonely child, must have basked in the glow of her parents' happiness. To have them both together at once, and all three of them with nothing to do but enjoy themselves in each other's company, there was riches! There is a sad comment in one of Jawaharlal's letters about his thirteen-year-old daughter. Kamala, in spite of many illnesses, had at least had her growing time in peace, and she still looked ridiculously young. Indira had never truly had a childhood at all, and her face showed it. "Kamala has often been taken for my daughter. But what do you say to Indu being taken for the mother! This has happened repeatedly."

Life for the next three years followed much the same pattern as before. Jawaharlal spent much time in prison, Kamala much time in the hospital. The fight for India's future flared by fits and starts, was pursued through commissions and talks and conferences, from Westminster to Delhi.

Whatever happens to a country, people still have to grow up, and through these years Indira got her schooling very much by fits and starts too. She has said that she cannot remember how many schools she went to in India altogether; there were times when the next step was left for her to arrange by herself, because everybody else was in prison or in the hospital. The best of the schools was one in Poona, run by a little gnome of a woman called "Auntie" Vakil. The three little Pandit girls, the youngest only three years old, were sent there too, because both their parents were in jail. Faced in those difficult years with an assortment of girls from every sort of background in India, "Auntie" solved some of their problems and her own by sending the older ones out to do social work. Indira worked in the slums among the *harijans*, the untouchables. From her father she inherited a total lack of caste consciousness, and in this, like him, she followed Gandhi, although as she grew up, there were many ways in which she too

felt impatient with the little man. It is very difficult to
see eye to eye with a saint.

But, in prison or out, the chief influence was still
her father, what he thought, what he said, what he
wanted of her. Her view of the world was shaped by
him and by the book he wrote for her, *Glimpses of
World History*. He began it on her thirteenth birthday,
before Motilal's death, while he was in Naini.

"On your birthday you have been in the habit of
receiving presents and good wishes. Good wishes you
will still have in full measure, but what present can I
send you from Naini Prison? My presents cannot be
very material or solid. They can only be of the air
and of the mind and spirit, such as a good fairy might
have bestowed on you—things that even the high walls
of prison cannot stop."

It worried him to think then of the odd, unbalanced
upbringing she was having. Picketing cloth-merchants'
shops was experience of a kind, no doubt, but it was not
all that you would wish for in the way of an education.
He thought of the years to come : whatever happened to
the daughter of the Nehrus, it was likely that she
would have some part in the future of her country. She
must be educated.

And so he began, in a stop-and-start uneven fashion,
to write for her the history of the world, the history
of man's progress. He had very few books at hand;
he had H. G. Wells's *Outline of World History* and
he had the memories he had accumulated in his own

years of reading. It is not a scholarly work. No one
would read it to get a factual, objective account of
history. But it is a superb book; it gives a bird's-eye, or
rather a prisoner's-eye, view of the whole sweep of
events since the beginning of time. It is the view of a
noble mind judging the onward progress of the human
race and judging his own place in it, and it cannot fail
to move the reader. Nehru wrote three books in prison,
in fact: *Glimpses of World History*, his own *Autobiography*, and *The Discovery of India*. The following par-
agraph comes from the last of them but might as well
have been the preface to the first.

"What is my inheritance? To what am I heir? To all
that humanity has achieved during tens of thousands
of years, to all that it has thought and felt and suffered
and taken pleasure in, to its cries of triumph and its
bitter agony of defeat, to that astonishing adventure of
man which began so long ago and yet continues and
beckons to us. To all this and more in common with all
men. But there is a special heritage for those of us in
India, not an exclusive one, for none is exclusive and all
are common to the race of man, one more especially
applicable to us, something that is in our flesh and
bones, that has gone to make us what we are and what
we are likely to be."

He wrote his history book quite as much for himself
as for Indira. She did not even get the letters. They
piled up beside him in prison, and when he finally
came out, he brought out with him half a million words.
But just the writing of it made her seem very close.

Often he wonders whether he is boring her, whether the long absence is making them grow away from each other. Sometimes the letters follow each other daily for several weeks. Sometimes he has moods when the make-believe fails and he writes nothing.

"Lately I have felt little inclined to write these letters, which no one sees but myself. They are pinned together and put away to await the time, months or years hence, when perhaps you may see them. Months or years hence! when we meet again, and have a good look at each other, and I am surprised to find how you have grown and changed. We shall have plenty to talk of and to do then, and you will pay little attention to these letters. There will be quite a mountain of them by that time, and how many hundreds of hours of my prison life will be locked up in them!"

When at last she did read them, what a lot she must have learned about the father she adored. Although he wrote simply, he was never hypocritical; he had too much respect for her integrity for that. So his moods and troubles and opinions went down just as they occurred.

"I am afraid the next world does not interest me. My mind is full of what I should do in this world, and if I see my way clearly here, I am content."

"Whether Alexander was a really great man or not is a doubtful matter. He is certainly no hero of mine . . . He left nothing solid behind him in his empire— not even proper roads—that he had built. Like a meteor

in the sky he came and went, and left little of himself
behind except a memory."

"What a burden our peasantry have carried these
many years! And let us not forget that we, who have
prospered a little, have been part of that burden. All of
us, foreigner and Indian, have sought to exploit that
long-suffering *kisan* and have mounted on his back."

"I am an 'habitual' now, in the language of the
prison, and that many times over, and I am used to gaol
life. It is a strange contrast to my life outside, of work
and activity and large gatherings and public speaking
and a rushing about from place to place. Here all is
different; everything is quiet, and there is little movement, and I sit for long intervals, and for long hours I
am silent. The days and the weeks and the months pass
by, one after the other, merging into each other, and
there is little left to distinguish one from the other. And
the past looks like a blurred picture with nothing stand-
ing out. Yesterday takes one back to the day of one's
arrest, for in between is almost a blank with little to
impress the mind. It is the life of a vegetable rooted to
one place, growing there without comment or argument, silent, motionless . . . One gets used to everything in time, even to the routine and sameness of gaol.
And rest is good for the body; and quiet is good for the
mind; it makes one think."

Indira was nearly sixteen before the complete series
of letters, and her father, came out of prison together.
But this time it was a short and uneasy freedom, more
wearing on the spirit than the finality of jail. "I've

been waiting for you a long time," he said to the police
officer who drove up to the verandah of Anand
Bhawan five months and thirteen days later. Five
months and thirteen days, of which every day might
be the last, and every day brought difficult decisions.
How to act? How many speeches to make when the
next speech might precipitate rearrest? How to govern
one's actions and walk the tightrope between cowardice
and foolhardiness? No wonder that during those five
months his temperament began to fray around the
edges ("You're getting cattish," said a friend).

In this atmosphere Indira's sixteenth birthday came
and went and 1933 struggled to its end. Swaruprani
was ill and confined to her room, waited on by the
devoted Bibi Amma. Kamala, in the ups and downs of
tuberculosis, was much more ill than any of them
would accept. She should have been in the hospital in
Calcutta where a specialist had some new treatment, but
how could she go when every day might see the black
police car turn in through the Anand Bhawan gates?
Let them stay together now; there would be time for
treatments in the uncertain future, when she was bound
to be alone again.

And for that inevitable time ahead, what about
Indira's education? She was coming up for matricula-
tion at her Poona boarding school, and what about the
next step? Was there enough money for a next step at
all? To meet this problem, all Kamala's jewelry, and
the family silver that remained, was sold and Anand
Bhawan was stripped of several cartloads of expend-

able bits and pieces. The family bank balance looked
healthier than it had for some time. Kamala regretted
the jewelry; she never wore it, but it would have been
nice for Indira's wedding. Indira was not impressed,
though. So it was sold and the money earmarked for
her to go to England to the university one day. But she
was only sixteen and the time for that step was not yet.
She must get the best of the East before she went
westward.

"I was wholly against her joining the regular official
or semi-official universities for I disliked them. The
whole atmosphere that envelops them is official, oppressive and authoritarian. They have no doubt produced
fine men and women in the past, and they will continue
to do so. But these few exceptions cannot save the universities from the charge of suppressing and deadening
the fine instincts of youth. Santiniketan offered an
escape from this dead hand, and so we fixed upon it,
although in some ways it was not so up to date and well-
equipped as the other universities."

On January 15, 1934, Jawaharlal and Kamala were
booked on the night train from Allahabad to Calcutta.
They would arrange for Kamala's hospital treatment
and visit Santiniketan at the same time. It was a curi-
ously oppressive afternoon for January and the dogs
were howling. The garden at Anand Bhawan was full
of white figures; it was Magh Mela time and there was
always a rush of pilgrims to see Jawaharlal if he was at
home to be seen. He stood on the verandah with one

hand on a pillar, talking to the crowding groups. The pillar began to shake.

"An earthquake! Come out!" cried old Bibi Amma, hobbling energetically out of her little house. A few tiles slid with a crash into the garden. Then the quake subsided and a buzz of conversation rose. Presently the crowd drifted off, Kamala came downstairs, the packing finished, and a little later they were on the train.

As it rattled down to Calcutta, 500 miles away, the Nehrus slept in their berths, quite unaware that they were crossing an area torn to shreds by one of the world's great earthquakes. The shock that had knocked off tiles in Allahabad had collapsed cities like paper bags in Bihar. A million houses came down, and twenty thousand people, as near as anybody could ever guess, were dead underneath them. So complete was the destruction that for a while no one outside the area knew anything about it. The Nehrus spent several days in Calcutta, and news at last began to trickle through. When they returned, by daylight train, through Bihar, they saw with horror what they had missed before.

Jawaharlal had made three public speeches in Calcutta, all of them antigovernment, all, he was aware, bringing rearrest that much nearer. Then he went off to the earthquake-stricken areas for ten days and came home limp and gray with strain. Next day the police car arrived with a warrant which had followed him from Calcutta, and back he went there, to stand trial and be given his seventh prison sentence, for two years this time. For once at their farewell, Kamala's spirit failed and she collapsed in his arms; never had the parting seemed so desolating. "Of the many hard lessons that I had learnt, the hardest and the most painful now faced me: that it is not possible in any vital matter to rely on any one. One must journey through life alone; to rely on others is to invite heartbreak."

Jawaharlal was a mature man of forty-five when he wrote that. It might also have been the philosophy of the thin dark-eyed girl who got off the train at Bolpur for her first university term, utterly composed as she always was, ordinary, not noticeable in the crowds of teenagers. The campus she arrived at was a ramble of low buildings on high bare ground. The sun beats hard on bare earth here most of the year until the rains make the rice fields green again. But the buildings were interspersed with trees which cast black shadows, very pleasant against the glare.

This was Santiniketan, the House of Peace, built and growing over the years under the hand of Rabindranath Tagore, the poet-philosopher, and here Indira was suddenly aware of a security that neither her home nor any of her many schools had yet given her. Here was peace, here was wholeness, the wholeness of a philosophy that saw all life as one. And here was the great Tagore himself, still young in heart at seventy-three (by a strange coincidence, he had been born on the same day as her grandfather Motilal: the one in Calcutta, the other in Agra). Superbly imposing, his wise, kind, handsome face with a flowing white beard, his personality larger than life, he spoke English and Bengali with equal power and grace, his voice deep and musical. "There has been no one like him anywhere on our globe for many and many centuries," said one of his followers. "He is the most Universal, the most encompassing, the most complete human being I have ever known." In the generous shadow of this personality Indira was to spend the only months of her youth that she has ever spoken of with enthusiasm.

Rabindranath Tagore was born into a rich and cultured family, as huge and rambling as the enormous Calcutta house they all lived in. Calcutta was the capital then of British India, and from an early age the little Rabindranath, listening to his much older brothers, was aware that the shades of some Westernized and mercantile prison house were closing in on a society that once upon a time had existed in India, "a society hospitable, sweet with the old-world aroma of natural kindliness, full of a simple faith and the ceremonial poetry of life." Whether this golden age ever in fact existed does not matter—a boy grew up yearning for it. He longed too for the "illimitable magic of land, water and air." The trees "made my heart wistful with the invitation of the forest." This longing was intensified by his early days spent in the midst of a swarm of unimaginative servants, and by just one holiday away from the city, when he found the magic of the ebb and flow of the Ganges, the boats, the wide sky, the changing colors and flying shadows of a riverside landscape.

He hated school passionately. "Possibly my suffer-

ing was unusual, greater than that of most other children. The non-civilized in me was sensitive: it had a
great thirst for colour, for music, for the movement of
life. Our city-built education took no heed of that
living fact. It had its luggage-van waiting for branded
bales of marketable result." A bright spark was his
discovery of a Bengali translation of *Robinson Crusoe:*
life could be as he dreamed it, it could be free and full
of the adventure of improvising as one went along.

Rabindranath grew into a poet. He wrote poetry,
plays, stories, essays, criticism. He became one of the
great figures of India, the quintessence of the artistic
Bengali way of life, as Gandhi was the quintessence of
the Gujrati way of life from the other side of the subcontinent. Jawaharlal said of them: "I have always
been fascinated by these two towering personalities
. . . Tagore was the poet and the singer; Gandhi was
the man of action, the true revolutionary, single-
minded in his aim and going as the arrow from the bow.
To Tagore poetry and music were the essence of life
which gave it rhythm, and his philosophy was one of
living in harmony with nature. Gandhi did not talk or
perhaps read much of poetry or art, and yet his life
. . . was a poem in action." In 1913 Tagore won the
Nobel Prize for literature, and as he had already
founded Santiniketan, the prize was used to finance it.

This "House of Peace" began as a school for boys,
built on the site at Bolpur which his father had used as
an *ashram*, a retreat. Here he put his ideas into practice:
"Modern man is busy building his cage, fast develop-

Motilal Nehru with his wife Swaruprani and their son Jawaharlal, about 1895.

Jawaharlal Nehru with his wife Kamala and their daughter Indira.

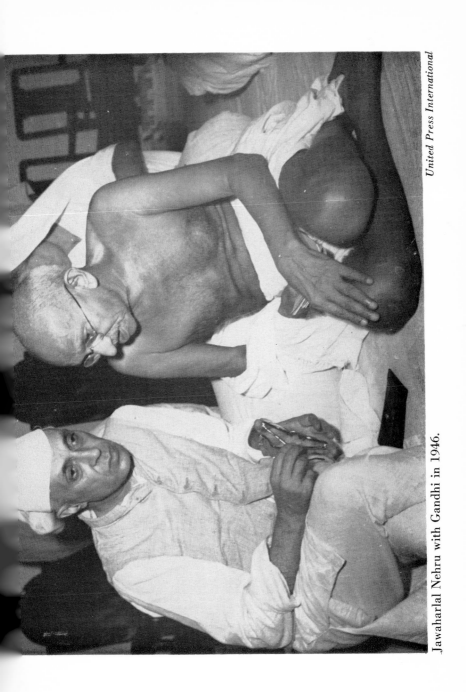

Jawaharlal Nehru with Gandhi in 1946.

Rabindranath Tagore, poet and teacher of Indira Gandhi.

Indira Gandhi in New York, 1949, with Nehru and his sister, Vijaya Lakshmi Pandit, at that time Indian ambassador to the United States.

Nehru, President Kennedy, and Indira Gandhi in 1961.

Indira Gandhi in 1959. She had just become the president of the
Congress Party. Behind her is a picture of Mohandas Gandhi, no
relation but an influential friend and advisor.

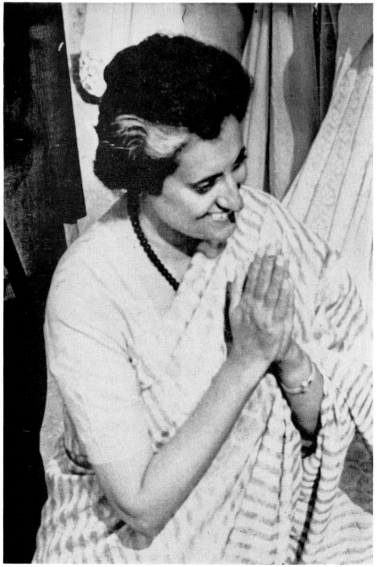

Madame Prime Minister, 1966. She is giving the traditional Indian greeting to a group of her countrymen.

ing his parasitism on the monster, *Thing*, which he
allows to envelop him on all sides."

Visitors found the Santiniketan boys learning in the
open air, writing their compositions in the top branches
of the sal trees if they liked. Everywhere there was
music, poetry, movement, a bareness which was plain
but not pinching, a warmth of understanding between
students and teachers. Sometimes when the full moon
shone like a cool white sun, boys and masters would
take off for long night walks across the country, sing-
ing as they went. Tagore, like a better kind of Squeers,
would suddenly break off an English lesson to send
every boy racing for the top of the mango trees to rip
off a leaf and bring it back to him. "Now you understand the English word 'to tear.' "

As with all progressive schools, Tagore at first got an
overlarge number of misfits, the naughty boys whose
fathers used this as a last resort which it could not do
any harm to try. They were allowed to climb and
scramble and splash and swim and raise cain in the open
air until they worked themselves on to an even keel. "It
was my ambition that I would make the children
happy."

Later the school developed side by side with a student center, Visva-Bharati. This, as Tagore saw it, was
to be a sort of International University where the best
minds of East and West should meet and cross-fertilize.
Here was to be a rich atmosphere, a full community
life of pupils and teachers, coeducation and a cosmo-
politan organization. Everything as far as could be

from what Tagore called "the education factory—
lifeless, colourless, dissociated from the context of the
universe, within white walls staring like eyeballs of the
dead."

This was the one university in India, Jawaharlal
Nehru felt, which could not be accused of "suppressing
and deadening the fine instincts of youth," although
it was "not so up-to-date and well-equipped as the other
universities." In 1934, when Indira went there, it
offered courses in most of the languages and cultures of
patchwork India. You could study Buddhist or Hindu
philosophy, take courses in Bengali, Hindi, Urdu,
Sanskrit, or English literature. There was dancing and
craft and folksong from every province between
Kanchenjunga and Cape Comorin. The students,
though naturally Bengalis predominated, included
Parsis and Punjabis, Gujratis and Singhalese, Rajas-
thanis and Assamese, Hindus, Musalmans, Sindhis and
Suratis. The staff was as mixed as the student body.
Distinguished foreigners—Austrian, English, Czech,
American, Russian, Norwegian, or French—came for
longer or shorter periods, caring less for the salaries
(financially the school was always on a razor's edge)
than for the privilege of working in Tagore's world of
high endeavor and imagination.

"I refuse to think," he said, "that the twin spirits of
the East and West, the Mary and the Martha, can
never meet to make perfect the realisation of truth. In
spite of our material poverty and the antagonism of
time I wait patiently for this meeting."

On Indira the effect was profound. In her sixteen
short years, politics had been the hard center of life,
the inescapable framework. "Tagore," she discovered,
"showed that art and life are integrated." Indira, basically an artistic personality, found that she could re-
spond to the arts without betraying the national cause
to which she was dedicated.

Switzerland and England

Indira stayed at Santiniketan less than a year. The next spring Rabindranath Tagore was writing to Jawaharlal: "It is with a heavy heart we bade farewell to Indira, for she was such an asset in our place. I have watched her very closely and have felt admiration for the way you have brought her up. Her teachers, all in one voice, praise her and I know she is extremely popular with the students. I only hope things will turn for the better and she will soon return here and get back to her studies."

What had turned for the worse was her mother's health. Kamala was already dying a consumptive's slow death when Indira went to Bolpur, although no one was ready to realize it. Jawaharlal, imprisoned at first at Calcutta, was later transferred to a healthier, cooler jail in the hills, and from there he had been released for eleven uneasy days in the summer because Kamala was very ill. Indira too was summoned to her mother's side. A sad meeting: it seemed that the family was only blown together on gusts of distress and then blown apart again.

Kamala rallied, and, the immediate danger over, Jawaharlal went back to prison and to "the longest and most damnable thirty days that I had ever experienced" as he struggled with the realization that perhaps indeed he was going to lose his wife just when every meeting seemed to bring more understanding of each other. "We came ever nearer to each other, and to leave her was a wrench. We met only to be parted. And sometimes I thought with anguish that a day might come when the parting was for good."

Indira went back to Santiniketan. Soon, however, it was decided that the last hope for Kamala lay in Europe, in a return to a sanatorium in south Germany or Switzerland, and Indira, naturally, was the person to go with her.

It was a grim time. The only brightness in the family situation was that Krishna, a year married, had a son, the first boy in the family since Jawaharlal himself. "Cheerio get well soon darling and bring the howling infant here for display and criticism," Jawaharlal wired cheerfully from prison. But when he did see the baby soon afterward, it was when they all met to say goodbye to Kamala.

Swaruprani was there too, frail, only partly recovered from a stroke. Krishna and her husband and the baby were there, and Jawaharlal, as usual under police

escort. Kamala and Indira drove away down the hill on
the first leg of their long journey half across the world.
They had all tried so hard to be cheerful, but Krishna
noticed that when Jawaharlal turned away from them
to get into the police car, his drooping shoulders and
unspringy step were saying what he would not let his
face express. He was facing the knowledge that he had
probably seen his wife for the last time.

But it was not so. When her health did not improve in
Europe, he was released, six months short of his full
sentence, so that he could join her, and the family were
together once more : more or less together, since Kamala
was in her hospital room, Jawaharlal living in the village nearby so that he could walk up each day to see
her, Indira at school once more not far away.

At this moment in her life, for once, someone looked
squarely at Indira instead of through or past her, and
saw very clearly what was happening to her. Agatha
Harrison was Gandhi's representative in England, and
she was largely responsible for getting Jawaharlal released to be with Kamala in her last months. She
had gone out to Switzerland and had written to
Gandhi what she found there, a young girl three
thousand miles from home, looking after her dying
mother while her father fretted in jail. "What a pa-
thetic figure—though young in years—old beyond
her years in experience and suffering. I went up to see
Mrs. Nehru who looked to me desperately ill and terribly weak. I only stayed a minute for she needs to
husband every ounce of strength. The rest of that day

I spent with Indira—and we got to know each other and I heard something of her life."

The eyewitness was on the spot again when Jawaharlal arrived and when he stood talking to the doctor at the sanatorium. "What touched and moved me most —was to watch this Father and daughter together. Indira was holding tight to his arm, every now and then rubbing her head against his shoulder and some of the 'years' that I had noticed the day before seemed to have slipped away, and she was a different person."

For several months more Kamala's disease followed its typically halting progress. Over and over again the flame spurts up to give an illusion of light and warmth, but each time it sinks, the wick is perceptibly shorter. Still, there were times when she could be left for a while, and in the winter Jawaharlal went over to London to pick up old threads of friendship, taking Indira with him. She met people who for her father's sake would be kind to her when the time came for her to study in England. This had always been the plan for her education, interrupted though it had been. After India, England. In the future, India was going to need the best of all the worlds, and no false patriotism would make the Indians reject what the West had to offer. Besides, in spite of his long tussle with the British raj, Jawaharlal in one sense was still more English than Indian.

Back in Switzerland, they heard that Jawaharlal had been elected president of Congress once again. The Government of India Act, recently passed, had

changed the look of things considerably. India now had
some kind of self-government—not enough, not what
the nationalists were fighting for, but still there was
peace, and no more danger of prison, at least for the
moment. Jawaharlal was needed to take up his country's political life once more. Should he go?

Kamala generously urged him to go. She was a little
better, and with the air services moving more fre-
quently, India and Switzerland were much nearer than
they had once been. He did go, but not quite as they
had hoped. In the end, Kamala died almost unexpect-
edly, and Jawaharlal flew back in time to take up his
post, gray, desolate, and much older, beside him on the
plane the casket of his wife's ashes. At least it was
politics and not prison that he returned to; he could
plunge head over ears into activity to try to muffle his
loneliness.

And Indira, as self-contained as her neat suitcases,
was on the doorstep of an English boarding school,
among the shrill chatter of a hundred English school-
girls, carrying with her the memories of her mother's
last days. Kamala had drifted gently at the end, sometimes hearing voices calling from a long way off, sometimes seeing a figure at the door. She had died with
Jawaharlal on one side of her bed and Indira on the
other. And Indira settled into the screeching hubbub of
dining room and dormitory and the business of reading
for her entance exam to Somerville College, Oxford.

Badminton was not quite like other schools of its
type. Its headmistress belonged to the Women's Inter-

national League for Peace and Freedom, which among other things had provided Gandhi with some of his most useful workers. Indira's aunt, Mrs. Pandit, was also a member, and so the connection had been made. At a time when the prospectuses of most English boarding schools did not go much further than assuring parents of their suitability for "the daughters of gentlemen," Badminton expressed its intentions quite differently: "The questions of the day are brought to the notice of the girls in the hope that they will make the habit of forming independent judgements on matters of national and international importance. There is a branch of the League of Nations Union in the school, and whenever possible, arrangements are made for the school journey to include attendance at the Annual League of Nations Union Junior School at Geneva."

So there must have been much kindness and sympathy from girls whose education purposely turned their minds outward from domestic to world problems. There may even have been understanding of the kind that Jawaharlal at Harrow complained he could not get from English schoolboys: at least two of Indira's contemporaries in the sixth form were Indians—one of them is now a Communist member of the Indian parliament.

Even so, this was 1936 and the place was unalterably British. A gold and gray house of Cotswold stone in a garden which had been nearly two hundred years growing: terraces of roses, wistaria trailing over stone balustrades, green lawns, and clipped yew trees. The weather that summer was unalterably British too.

Rain, icy winds, thunderstorms alternating with patches of teasing blue sky and hot spells that were over almost before they began.

The school diary, which recorded notable events:

> "May 14th.   Lecture by Mr. Aston No. 6. 'The French Cathedrals.'
>
> May 23rd.   Cricket Match v. Fry's XI.
>
> May 25th.   Mid-Somerset Musical Festival of Bridgwater. Advanced and Middle-school Pipe Bands."

What did Indira feel about it all? Nobody knew then and nobody is likely to find out now. Although she often wore a sari among short-skirted classmates (this was not special treatment; the sixth-form girls were allowed to wear their own clothes), her protective coloring was as strong as ever. Nobody saw her looking lonely or miserable, although her face, until she smiled, was cast in sad lines which would never be eradicated. Nobody knew whether she longed for the warm dusty campus of Santiniketan or the spacious coolness of Anand Bhawan. Nobody knew how much she thought about her mother, or her father, or India. She was invariably courteous, and kind, and gracious, in a way that set her apart from gangling contemporaries, but this was not surprising, as she was older than most of them in years as well as maturity. They remembered a particular charm, but they did not feel that they knew her well. "She was a schoolgirl, just an ordinary schoolgirl with a nice sense of humour."

There were occasional flashes. "After all that the British have done to you, why do you Indians still come here to be educated?" her headmistress asked her. The answer was quick. "Because the better we know you the better we can fight you," said Indira with her charming smile.

As the year wore on, her letters to her father indicated that she could not help feeling "an alien in this complacent English society." It was almost precisely what Jawaharlal had written from Harrow thirty years before. But there is no evidence that Oxford, where she went the following year to read for a degree in history, was to Indira what Cambridge had been to her father. Times were very different; the shadow of war was over Europe, an uneasy peace over India. Moreover, ill health plagued her through her late teens and early twenties. She left her Oxford course unfinished, as all her formal education had been left unfinished.

In India things were moving. The Government of India Act of 1935 had provided for a parliamentary form of democracy in which Indians were to take their full part in the provinces, though not in the central government. The constitution itself was sound enough; India's present constitution is based on it. But it was not independence or anything near it. Defense, external affairs, all the most important areas of power were reserved for the Viceroy and, beyond him, for the government in London.

Congress at first decided not to cooperate: its mem-

bers would not seek election under what Nehru called a
"new charter of slavery." But Congress as a whole had
been too long in the wilderness not to long for some
opportunity actually to rule, and they changed their
minds. Nehru, their president in 1936 and again in
1937, had to change his mind too. His election campaign, in which he spoke for the party and not for
himself, was a prodigious feat of strength. He covered
50,000 miles in five months, using every form of
transport from aircraft to camel and canoe. Probably ten million people saw him speak, or at least saw a
tiny white figure in the distance, and this was enough
for most of them, for he had emerged not only as a
great leader but as a beloved one, and never happier
than in the middle of enormous crowds, from whom he
drew a positive strength.

Now undoubtedly he was by far the most important person in India, with the exception of Gandhi, but
the two were too different to be compared. Their relationship remained a deep and involved one. Nehru
needed Gandhi as much as he had needed his father;
but politically he agreed with him less and less. He
wanted socialism, modernization, industrialization;
Gandhi's spinning wheel simply would not do as the
symbol of the new India.

The unhappiest feature of those years was the increasing bitterness of the struggle between Congress
and the Muslim League. It was not quite a straight
struggle between Hindu and Moslem because Nehru
fought with all his strength to keep Congress as an all-

India party, without religious overtones. But it is difficult to do things in India without religious overtones,
and his secular views were shared by few of his followers. The idea of Pakistan, as a separate Moslem state,
was slowly hardening, though no one can point to the
moment when it became inevitable.

Indira at Oxford, though far from home, was at least
more in touch with Indian affairs than she could have
been at Badminton. She spent two vacations at home,
and her father came over for several months in 1938.
She met Indian students: among them was a friend
from Allahabad, Feroze Gandhi (no relation of the other
Gandhi), a Parsi student at the London School of Eco-
nomics. Feroze had been a schoolboy worker under
Kamala during the months in 1931 when all the men
were in prison. He had conceived a great admiration for
her then, as so many people did when they knew her—
so much so that he had made a special trip to Switzerland to visit her when she was ill.

In London the India League was the center for ex-
patriate Indians and sympathetic British. Indira was
often to be found in a corner, quietly addressing
envelopes. As Nehru's daughter she could have had
as much limelight as she wanted—even while she
was a schoolgirl at Badminton, local groups had pursued her with requests. It was not from lack of interest in India's problems that she preferred to stay in the
background, or from lack of ability. She preferred to
address envelopes, and people simply forgot to notice
whether she was there or not, as half the time her own

family forgot to notice whether she was there or not.

From the time she left India with her mother in 1935 to her final return in 1941 was a lapse of six years. She left as a girl of seventeen and came back a young woman of twenty-three. By that time most of the world was at war, including India as a British possession. But though many thousands of Indian troops fought with the Allies, Congress once more refused to cooperate in a battle which they felt had nothing to do with their country; their leaders, Nehru of course first of all, were once more sent off to prison, this time for the duration.

When this happened, Indira was no longer in England. Her health had failed, and, with her mother's example before her, she wisely took herself off to a sanatorium in Switzerland. At the end of several monotonous months, better in body but strained in mind, all she wanted to do was to get back to India. She could not bear to be an exile any longer.

"You must know that Indu has left Switzerland," wrote Nehru from prison in December 1940, "and is trying to get back to India. The journey is a roundabout one. I think one goes by Antibes from Geneva to Marseille, or probably beyond. Then by air to Barcelona, Lisbon and London. From London she will have to come by sea convoy. It is not at all easy to get passages and there are long waiting lists. She will have to wait at least a month, maybe two or more. So even if all goes well, she is not likely to reach Bombay before the end of February. More likely March." (In fact, it was well into May, after a tedious journey. At one moment she was stuck in Lisbon, short of cash, and gave English lessons to tide herself over. But she got home.) "I am glad she has decided to return. There are all manner of risks and dangers of course but it is better to face them than to feel isolated and miserable. If she wants to return then she must do so or take the consequences."

Wedding and War

For the Nehru family the wedding of Indira Prya-darshini to Feroze Gandhi was the bright event of 1942. For once they flocked to Anand Bhawan and found it lighted and gay, almost as though Motilal might come beaming out to the verandah and take them into the charmed circle of his warmth. "I had travelled by the same route innumerable times during the past nine and a half years," said Krishna, "but each time I had felt a little uneasy, wondering what news would greet me on my arrival, for something unexpected and unpleasant always happened. Either mother was suddenly taken ill or Jawahar had been arrested, and so on."

This time their meeting was to be without a shadow, although, let it be said at once, nobody was quite happy about Indira's choice. Feroze was a Parsi, and whatever they might say, none of them liked the mixing of races and religions. "Would you let your daughter marry a Parsi?" was a question with emotional overtones even in this home of liberalism. But the Nehru women had long outgrown arranged marriages, and Indira had made her own choice. She was twenty-four, and she had had years of practice in making up her own mind when there was nobody around to make it up for her. Also, she got unexpected support from her grandmother, Kamala's mother, a most orthodox old lady who suddenly raised the flag for unorthodoxy and supported her granddaughter in the face of anybody's opposition.

"In fact, the entire Indian nation disapproved," Indira said cheerfully in later years. Jawaharlal's daughter was India's property, and the letters poured in, mostly scurrilous. Even Gandhi disapproved——the other Gandhi, the Mahatma. Indira had a good many arguments with him on the subject, for Bapu was Bapu to the whole family and for twenty years they had laid all their problems at his sandaled feet. Long after, Indira mentioned this in the course of a radio interview and the interviewer expressed surprise. Surely, he said, mixed marriages were just what Gandhi *did* approve? Getting rid of the caste barriers? Doing away with differences?

Indira considered a moment: "I think the principle of it appealed to him," she said. "But he didn't really like them." This disconcerting habit of hitting the nail on

the head in unvarnished words of one syllable is perhaps the reason why some people have doubted that
she will ever make a successful politician.

March in Allahabad is a pleasant month, not yet too
hot, and the astrologers had chosen the fourth as a
favorable day. For once, everybody was out of prison;
the detainees had been let out halfway through their
sentences. And for once, for one day, Indu was the
center of everybody's attention. She was always the
apple of her father's eye, but she was too quiet and self-
effacing to stand out in a family of strong and conflict-
ing personalities. But you cannot ignore the bride at a
wedding. One gets the impression that the aunts and the
cousins looked at her clearly that day and were surprised to find what a beautiful young woman she was.

The house was full of presents. They had arrived
from all over the country, and a good many had been
promptly sent back again. It seemed a good rule to
accept nothing except from personal friends: you never
quite know what invisible political string is attached to a
diamond brooch.

The house was full of children too: the three Pandit
girls agog with interest for the first family wedding
they had taken part in, and Krishna's two little boys.
Indira wore a pale pink sari made from a length of
khadi spun and woven by her father in jail. It was
edged with silver embroidery. Dark and pensive, light-
ing up with her sudden smile, she looked like a
princess. The wedding ceremony was to take place on
the round verandah of Anand Bhawan, and here the

mats had been laid for the close relations, and the sacred fire lighted. Beyond the verandah were chairs on the lawn, and beyond that, the pushing crowds of onlookers who had always thought of Anand Bhawan and the Nehrus as their own property.

Someone always cries at a wedding. You cannot gather a family together on rare occasions without having them look back to earlier occasions, counting the gaps in their ranks and the changes brought by time. Across the way stood the gaunt empty shell of the old Anand Bhawan, and the circle of mats had been laid just outside Swaruprani's old room and a few steps from where dear Bibi Amma had lived her hermit's life. More touching still was the empty mat at Nehru's side where Kamala, six years dead, should have sat to watch her daughter given away. The fire is the witness to the marriage ceremony, and it sputters brightly as the old priest feeds it with chips of sandalwood and drops of melted butter from a silver spoon. The smoke drifts out over the garden. At first the daughter sits beside her father, and then, officially given away, she moves around to sit beside her husband. The couple take their seven steps around the fire, repeating the ancient Sanskrit words:

*"By taking seven steps with me do thou become
    my friend.
By taking seven steps together we become friends.
I shall become thy friend.
I shall never give up thy friendship.*

Do thou never give up my friendship.
Let us live together and take counsel of one
    another."

The two of them are joined together by a scarf, and
then it is the girls' turn to swarm around, scattering
rose petals and repeating the traditional verses. On this
occasion the ceremony, for an Indian wedding, was
short; it was over in an hour and a half. Then the band
played, the conversation buzzed, the crowd of relations
gathered to the wedding breakfast.

Five months later the whole Nehru family was in
prison again, in the cleanest sweep of all. For a while
the younger Pandit girls, aged fifteen and thirteen,
were holding the fort alone at Anand Bhawan except
for an old servant or two. Their mother and father,
their uncle Jawaharlal, Feroze and Indira, even Lekha,
their seventeen-year-old sister, had all been locked up.
Krishna, in Bombay, had kept out of trouble because
her children were only six and seven years old, but her
husband had gone with the others. Japanese armies
were knocking at India's back door, and the authorities
had no time for anything but stern measures. In the
crisis, Gandhi had called upon the British to "quit
India," now, at once. Congress rallied behind him, and
60,000 disaffected Indians were put back into jail.

Jawaharlal and Raja, Krishna's husband, were
arrested at the house in Bombay. Indira helped to pack
their bags. Then she returned to Allahabad, and the
very night she arrived, while she was sleeping after the

long train journey, a convoy of five trucks pulled up outside Anand Bhawan at two in the morning to pick up her aunt, Mrs. Pandit. It was Mrs. Pandit's third experience of jail, and not unexpected, since she was an important member of the Congress Party and had in fact been their first woman cabinet minister. She hated jail. Jawaharlal settled down philosophically to his ninth imprisonment, which was also to be his longest, three years, until the war was over. But it was a different matter for a woman who did not know what had happened to her husband except that he had almost certainly been arrested too, somewhere; who was worried about her three young daughters. Also, instead of fairly civilized internment in the company of a dozen colleagues, with books and gardening and political discussion to while away the time, she was put into the women's half of Naini prison, where heat and dirt and things that crawled were much in evidence.

It was a relief to be joined a few days later first by Lekha, her eldest daughter, and then by Indira. The girls were full of spirits. Certainly Lekha was delighted with the adventure of prison; this set the seal on her growing up—she was really a worker for freedom now. She made light of discomforts and happily talked nonsense. She and Indira spent a long time planning a dinner party to be prepared from their rations, with Mrs. Pandit and the fourth occupant of the room as guests. They had four forks and one knife and argued whether the menu should be written in English or in French.

Lekha was not in for very long, and her mother was given a month's parole to arrange the family's affairs, which she did by sending two daughters to college in America (by troopship, alone, in the middle of a war) and the youngest to boarding school. Some members of the family protested loudly, and, of course, wrote to Jawaharlal about it, though what he was expected to do from Ahmadnagar Fort is not quite clear.

"We have never made 'safety first' our motto, and I hope we never will," was his answer. "It would be bad training indeed for the girls to be made to feel they must avoid risks and dangers at all costs."

Indira spent thirteen months in jail, for a great part of the time without letters or visits, and with no idea what had happened to her father or her husband. She had been married just five months. But she had learned the lessons of courage which her father had taught her so early. She did not fear and she did not hate and she could not be pushed around. Still, jail was a hard experience for someone of her fastidious and introspective temperament.

It was icy cold in winter and intolerably hot in summer. When the monsoon rains came, the prison barracks leaked. There were not only bats and an occasional snake, but endless flies, mosquitoes, and bugs. You name it, and it was crawling on the floor, flying through the air, or clinging to the water. The rations were of the poorest, often mixed with grit and dirt, stale or rancid. The tea seemed to come from some plant known only in jail. It was trying to be confined to so few clothes—six saris, which one had to wash by one-self in cold water. And even that was not so bad as trying to wash oneself successfully with one's clothes on at the communal tap—easy for her companions, who had learned the trick at the village well, but almost impossible for one brought up to a Western standard of plumbing. And there were small but intense humilia-tions. She loved mangoes—all the Nehrus did; they were connoisseurs of the different kinds. The first thing her father did when he heard that she was imprisoned was to try to make arrangements through Krishna to send her some mangoes. When the first lot arrived at last, all that she heard was that some petty official had im-pounded them and eaten them, and took pleasure in telling her so.

Later, things improved somewhat. Letters did arrive and were sent in return. Books got through. Feroze, though she did not see him, was no farther off than the men's block in the same prison. She heard from her father, and he was his usual philosophical self; he, after all, was serving his ninth prison sentence, she only her first. Perhaps she was able to remember and to learn from his experience: "One gets used to everything in time, even to the routine and sameness of gaol. And rest is good for the body; and quiet is good for the mind; it makes one think."

Prison did not hurt her health, and if it made her rub shoulders with some strange and new characters of whose existence she could hardly have been aware be-fore, this was perhaps not bad training either. She had wide tolerance, and this experience made it wider. And there were pleasures: a package of mangoes arrived at last, and she walked around it, extending the pleasure by anticipation—smelled them and touched them and almost hugged them, she wrote to her father.

A year after the great sweeping-up operation of August 1942, the family were out again, all but Nehru, who had to stay in until 1945, until the Allied victory over the Japanese ended the emergency. They did not get out scatheless; the most unlikely warrior was the casualty.

This was Ranjit Pandit, Nan's husband, a gentle scholar who spoke eleven languages, a Sanskrit expert, a musician, an adoring and adored father who had to die while his children were in America—"the human being nearest my heart," one of his daughters called him. He had everything, it seemed: money, good looks, an education in four universities, a beautiful wife, and such green fingers that he could keep even a prison yard full of flowers. But his health could not stand prison life, and although he was released on this occasion after a few months, it was not soon enough, and he died of pleurisy at the beginning of 1944.

"Bitterness filled me that he had to die," said his daughter Tara, "till I remembered that bitterness had been his most scorned enemy."

TEN

A Tryst with Destiny

The evening of August 14, 1947. Jawaharlal Nehru on his feet in parliament, holding, as only he could, every eye riveted. His speeches were always good. Sometimes, when the occasion demanded, they rose to great heights. This was such an occasion.

"Long years ago," he said, "we made a tryst with destiny, and now the time comes when we shall redeem our pledge, not wholly nor in full measure, but very substantially. At the stroke of the midnight hour, when the world sleeps, India will awake to life and freedom. A moment comes, which comes but rarely in history, when we step out from the old to the new, when an age ends, when the soul of a nation, long suppressed, finds utterance. It is fitting that at this solemn moment we take the pledge of dedication to the service of India and her people and to the still larger cause of humanity."

At midnight precisely, the members of the Assembly rose to their feet and took the solemn pledge of dedication to their new, free country. And then a conch shell blew loud and long, traditional herald of the dawn.

Outside, Delhi was going happily wild. Guns fired salutes, the temple bells rang till they cracked, fireworks whizzed and scattered stars over the sky, people danced and sang and cried slogans, Hindus and Moslems arm in arm. "We are one," they chanted, "we are one." Even the horses' legs were painted in stripes of the national colors.

All the next day, the official Independence Day, joy fizzed and crackled. The effigy of British imperialism was solemnly burned, but the individual Briton had never found himself so clapped on the back and patted and cheered, greeted with such fervor as a brother now that he was no longer trying to be a master. The most popular man in Delhi after Jawaharlal, who was mobbed to suffocation point wherever he showed himself, was Lord Mountbatten, yesterday the last Viceroy of India, today the first Governor-General of this newest member of the Commonwealth. Millions seemed to be out in the hot streets, and most of them getting in the way of the Governor-General's carriage with its six horses. Enormous crowds, warm and happy, surged out of police control, and a press photographer at one moment clicked his shutter on a scene that was typical of the day. The Mountbattens' open carriage moves slowly through the crowd toward whatever ceremony was next on the list. (Whatever it

was, they would certainly be late for it; the whole thing
was "the most successful ceremonial fiasco in India,"
said the Governor-General cheerfully.) On the hood of
the carriage, perched like a schoolboy, is the Prime
Minister, hitchhiking because his car had been hope-
lessly caught in the turmoil; and hanging on behind,
three women and a child who had also lost their way
and been rescued.

The day's celebrations were closed by the raising of
the new flag of India on the old Red Fort of Delhi.
Orange for courage, white for sacrifice, green for truth,
with the blue spinning wheel of Asoka across the
middle; as the flag rose slowly to the top of the staff
and unfurled, half a million people roared their
welcome.

But if the spinning wheel reminded people of Gandhi,
he was most conspicuously absent from the celebration,
holding a twenty-four hour fast in Calcutta. He
could not rejoice in an India which had agreed to
partition. For at the same time as India was born in
Delhi, Pakistan, Jinnah's Moslem state, was born in
Karachi. The struggles of all the years had resulted in
this.

India had not shrugged off its troubles with its old
allegiance—there were still the perennial problems of
food shortage, labor unrest, demands and pressures. The
war had brought many more people crowding into the
cities and had left them with living standards lower
than ever. But the question of all questions was: had

partition put a natural end to the communal jealousies
which time and again during the last year or two had
threatened to break out of their smoldering and con-
sume the subcontinent? Nehru hoped that it had. He
had always felt that the people of India, those white
crowds which flocked around him wherever he went,
did not want partition; that communal difficulties were
being fomented by jealous politicians, and that all this
would die down once freedom had come. In any case,
the British could not stay. If we must have civil war, we
must, was the feeling; just go away and leave us to
it.

They were left to it, and we are not yet far enough
from the events that followed to know whether they
were inevitable or not. If the mistakes can be laid at
any door, they must probably be laid at all doors—
British, Congress, Muslim League—and they went far
back down the years. The moment to save India from
partition was probably long before the word "partition" had been uttered by anyone.

Bengal and the Punjab were known to be the two
red-hot trouble spots, for it was in these two that the
partition lines ran, splitting through two ancient states
to satisfy the demands of religious enthusiasts. Eco-
nomics, language, culture—all were drastically divided.
Partition separated the growing jute from the mills
which processed it, the riverhead from the fields it
irrigated, the city from its grain. Roads and railways
were disrupted. The lines artificially drawn on a map

left millions of the mixed population on the wrong side, among neighbors who were meaningfully whetting their knives. But Gandhi was in Calcutta, in the heart of Bengal. There was no Gandhi in the Punjab.

In the middle of the Delhi celebrations, when all was peace and joy—even the slaughterhouses being closed for the day so that no living thing need be left out of the celebrations—up in the Punjab, relatively few miles away, behind a screen of cut telephone wires and poor communications, murder was stalking the towns and villages. In Amritsar, the sacred city of the Sikhs, the screams of murdered people could be heard again in Jallianwala Bagh, but now it was Indian against Indian, with a savage disregard for humanity that must have made General Dyer turn over in his grave.

Nehru went there to see and came back gray and sick. "My mind is full of horror," he said. This was what really hurt, after thirty years of Gandhi's teaching and the proud hopes of freedom fighters—that Indians could slaughter Indians with horrible relish.

Thirty miles from Amritsar, over the Pakistani border, in the city of Lahore, it was the Moslems sacking, looting, raping, burning, and murdering the Hindus.

And so the great exodus began. From the air you could see nothing but the winding ant columns of the refugees along the roads, and the smoke rising from burning villages. Sometimes the columns would meet and stop and fight, beating down the fields of grain that they were soon going to need desperately. There have been many horrible things perpetrated in the name of religion—never anything quite so horrible as this.

Delhi, its brief rejoicing over, began to bear the brunt of the new tragedy. The packed trains, chocked to the windows with humanity, people clinging to every vantage point and thick on the roofs as herrings in a shoal, began to come down from the Punjab. And these trains were stopped and raided by bands of Sikhs, as were the railway stations where the refugees waited for transport. They were attacked and gunned, and in the crowds every bullet could hardly help but go through three bodies. Women and children were stripped, raped, beaten. Bodies were left on the tracks, in the streets, heads and hands cut off, with grotesque and ghastly mutilations.

And the ones that got through—they had to be put somewhere. Delhi was ringed with refugee camps, bare, guarded concentrations of people without food or water, who presently began to die from cholera. Thousands more crowded into the city, and then riots broke out there, and there was killing in the streets of Delhi too. Indira caused consternation by setting up a soup kitchen for Moslem refugees in the garden of her father's house.

In Bengal there was Gandhi in his finest and most extraordinary hour. If there had been two Gandhis, another for the Punjab, things might have been different. But there was only one and he walked the streets of Calcutta. Wherever he went, some breath of sanity like a cool wind touched the mobs and quietened them. This was the power of love: Christ could have done it, St. Francis, Buddha; in the twentieth century, Gandhi.

It was not magic and it did not always work. One night an infuriated Hindu mob burst into his house, carrying a murdered man, screaming for vengeance. On this occasion it was Moslems who circled Gandhi, fending off the sticks and stones until the police arrived with tear gas. Gandhi acknowledged sadly that shouting at these rioters did no good, since they would not listen. Instead he tried the method that in the past had shaken both the British and the Indians. He went on a hunger fast, to last till he died or until Calcutta came to its senses. This was not Liverpool, or Chicago: five hundred policemen, including their British officers, went on a twenty-four-hour fast with him to show their support—even while they were hard at work with tear gas and *lathis* to restore order.

Suddenly peace fell over riot-torn Calcutta. Mob leaders hurried to Gandhi's bedside, to drop their weapons and promise him, in tears, that they would preserve the peace. Delegations of important merchants, Christians, Moslems, and Hindus, came too, to give their word that they would restore order wherever they could and do nothing to stir up trouble afterward. Nothing perhaps expresses the paradox of India so well; while violence could be so horrible (an American correspondent saw a child of six, carrying a baby, battered down in the street in front of him by men who then turned courteously and offered to escort him out of trouble), it could also be stopped by the power of one man. After three days Gandhi was able to break his fast, and Calcutta kept its promise. Whatever happened elsewhere in the next few months, Calcutta and Bengal were quiet, so quiet that Gandhi was able to go up to Delhi and do what he could to help there.

Nehru was not Gandhi: his power was not of that messianic kind. But what one man's courage could do, that he was doing. He had never shown fear in his life, nor been deflected because he was afraid of the consequences to himself, and his daughter now showed that she was a chip of that same block.

Indira was traveling by train to Delhi with her two small children, Rajiv and Sanjay, when at the station before Delhi, as the train pulled in, a riot was obviously erupting on the platform, a Moslem trying to board the train and a crowd of Hindus making sure that he would not. It was early in the morning; a young woman with a baby in her arms and a little boy of three is not by any standards expected to get embroiled in the affairs of humanity, but this young woman was Nehru's daughter.

"There was one of these sort of lynching incidents," she explained afterward with typical understatement. "It was a question of one against I don't know how many hundreds. I got out of the train, and in fact I would have done a great deal more except that I was in the process of dressing . . . But anyway I prevented that one man being killed." How? She made it all sound delightfully simple. "I just hung on to the toughest people I could see and I just said that, well, that it just can't be done, and the time he would have been killed they spent in arguing and then the train was leaving so the whole thing was settled."

Gandhi heard of it and taxed her with it. "Is this true?" She said it was. "Why didn't you tell me about it?" Indira explained that there wasn't anything to tell, it was just one of those things that happened. She hadn't thought about it, she had just done it.

The point of the story is not that it happened but that it astonished Gandhi, who had known her since she was a baby. Even he did not know what lay behind that shy, smiling façade. And yet it was not a façade, not intentionally. As a reporter said of her much later, she gave the impression of saying to you what came into her head, and yet you did not know her. On this occasion Gandhi asked her what she was doing, and she said she was working in a refugee camp, which was pretty unsatisfactory because there were plenty of people doing that and what she wanted was to help stop the trouble rather than just help in cleaning up afterward.

"All right," said Gandhi. "Go among the Moslems and see what you can do." Later he told her in so many words that he had not expected her to make any headway at all. It was not an easy assignment. The Hindus were furious; so were the Moslems. Nehru was bombarded with threatening letters: "It has happened to our daughters, what makes you think yours will be safe?" Going into the Moslem quarters, the little party would be surrounded by hostile faces, by thrown stones, dirty language, threats of rape and murder. Indira took it quite calmly; the ration system had broken down and she was there to try to restore it. What surprised her was the extent of the disorganization she encountered.

"They had had no food for some days, their ration shops were empty so we made a list of the number of ration shops and the proprietors, and came back to tell the authorities, saying that such and such ration shops have no rations, will you supply them? We thought that that part was finished and we could go on to something else, but we discovered that it wasn't finished, that in spite of our reporting, rations had not been supplied to them, so that we had to get hold of a truck and go where the rations were, measure them out ourselves and take them there and dole them out to the people."

By the end of 1947, things were better though still uncertain, particularly in Delhi, under the strain of so many Moslem refugees. If one had read no further in the story of India's independence, if it was a book with the last pages torn off, one would still feel that there was one last tragedy to come. For Gandhi was a mythic personage, and the pattern of the mythic story, the hero's death that others may live, is deeply and inevitably woven into human affairs.

In January 1948, Indira remembered afterward, she went to call on Gandhi, whom indeed she and her father saw nearly every day. With her went her cousin Tara Pandit and the small boy Rajiv. It was a cheerful meeting; they had brought a nosegay of flowers for Bapu, who made Rajiv laugh by offering to put them into his nonexistent hair and then attaching them instead to his anklet. The child trotted out into the garden to chase butterflies among the flower beds, and Gandhi talked cheerfully to the two young women; he was glad they had come, because he had had too many dull visitors that day.

Afterward, reconstructing that visit as everyone reconstructed their last sight of Bapu and tried to remember every second of it, Tara thought he had said, "I'm glad you came today, because the next time you see me it will be in a crowd." Looking back, that seemed significant, but Indira could not remember that any of his words had sounded like a premonition.

People wanted to believe that he had had a premonition. It would somehow make a little sense out of the totally senseless if he knew that he was going to die and went willingly.

The next day, as Gandhi went out to his prayer meeting, a young Hindu stepped out of the crowd and greeted him. Gandhi responded with the *namaste*, hands together. The young man pulled out a revolver and fired three times. "Oh, God," sighed the old man and died.

India rocked back on its heels. Its leader, its teacher, its savior was dead, killed by an Indian hand. "I have a sense of utter shame," said Nehru in a moving confession to the Assembly, "both as an individual and as the head of the Government of India that we should have failed to protect the greatest treasure that we possessed." Shaken to his depths by his sense of loss, Nehru went on the radio to tell the nation: "The light has gone out of our lives and there is darkness everywhere. I do not know what to tell you and how to say it. Our beloved leader, Bapu as we called him, the Father of the Nation, is no more. Perhaps I am wrong to say that. Nevertheless, we will not see him again as we have seen him for these many years. We will not run to him for advice and seek solace from him, and that is a terrible blow, not to me only, but to millions and millions in this country."

Mrs. Sarojini Naidu, the Grand Old Lady of India, said, however: "What is all the snivelling about? Would you rather he had died of decrepit old age or indigestion? This was the only death great enough for him."

Raj

For seventeen years Jawaharlal Nehru was Prime Minister of India and a power in world politics. He had always been a world politician, thinking in international terms even in the long years of the freedom movement. Now, the last of the trinity which newsmen irreverently used to call "the father, the son, and the holy ghost," his position in India and in the world at large was more that of a king than a prime minister. You can feel this in all the writings about Nehru—something of reverence, something of astonishment when he behaved like a common man. A sort of halo glimmered around him.

A recent writer on India has summed it up very well:

"This unique position was supported by a striking personality. The slight spare figure with mobile face and Gandhi capped head, contained an abounding en-

ergy which constantly astonished observers and a
magnetic personality which attracted while it com-
manded. Though an intellectual and an aristocrat to his
fingertips his eloquence could move the masses and he
derived strength as well as pleasure from contact with
them. His lightning tours made him known throughout
the country and his impatience was regarded as a kind
of divine discontent. Even his short temper was relished
by those who did not suffer from it. His integrity was
outstanding and a matter for awe. His catholic interest
in all sides of life, from gliding contests to trekking in
the hills, increased the sense of identification with the
people. A westerner in outlook, in taste, a secularist who
disclaimed the name of Hindu and disliked the title of
Pandit, he remained acceptable both to the orthodox and
the peasant because of his burning patriotism. Thus
Nehru not only had the national stage virtually to himself; with his antecedents and his gifts he was able to
dazzle and dominate the national audience that watched
him."

His problems were enormous, and at this short distance of time it is impossible to judge whether his
success in solving them was comparatively small or
comparatively large—whether anyone else could have
done better or whether no one else could have done half
as much.

For seventeen years he tried to bring some kind of
socialism by consent and not by domination into India,
and he made for that country a unique place as a sort of

bridge between East and West, which is perhaps to say no more than that he himself was a unique bridge between the East and the West. Certainly he saw non-alignment not as a withdrawal but as a very positive policy.

Under his leadership India worked her way through two five-year plans, with fair success. National income rose by 42 percent, income per head by 20 percent; these are impressive numbers.

He had some success too in giving equal legal rights to women, and some success in opening up education, though here again "success" is a relative term. Twenty-five percent of the population are now literate; this is not much, seen from one angle. Seen from another, it is a great deal: before 1947, only 10 percent were literate.

And so one can go on. The language problem remained unsolved and apparently insoluble. Nehru's attempts to make Hindi and English the two common languages of India were not successful, and the crevasse between north and south seems to widen. Language *is* a man; it is his parents, his memories, his culture, and above all his religion. The Tamil- and Telugu-speaking people of the south have rioted and killed for what they see as their rights of language; young men have poured gasoline over themselves and set it on fire. Feeling that can overflow like this wells up from a rock-bottom depth which is going to be hard to pacify or change.

In seventeen years Nehru did not solve the problem

of Kashmir, or improve relations with Pakistan, and relations with China had become much worse, since India sided with Tibet and gave the Dalai Lama shelter in 1959.

But we are not here to estimate the effect on India of Nehru's seventeen years in power, only the effect on his daughter. These were the important middle years of her life; she was thirty in 1947, forty-seven in 1964. It might have been better for her if her father had married again. There would have been many women willing and able to be his second wife, who would probably have made him happy and filled with grace and talent the position of first lady. Indira had the double burden of being both her father's first lady and also a political figure who might inherit her father's mantle. He never spared her. All her life he seems to have assumed, rather like a king, that there was no choice for his daughter in the matter of her own future, that she was born the daughter of the Nehrus, and that was that. There seems no truth in the gossipy stories that he was quietly grooming her all the time to take over his position, but there may well have been a silent feeling that being who she was she had no choice but to be deeply involved in her country's future, one way or another.

In 1945, when Nehru's last prison term ended and he took his place as an important political figure, he needed a hostess. There was Indira, and that was it. In spite of her fears that she could not do it, was not cut out for it, she simply had to. Her father assumed that she could and would, and since she had been trained for years in the stoical tradition of facing the lions, she did.

No wonder that under the strain her marriage creaked and cracked. Feroze was not an insignificant personage in his own right. He was a member of parliament, a bright spark of a ginger group which took it upon itself to root out corruption wherever it might be found, and there is always corruption to be found in Indian politics. Nehru did everything to make things easy for his son-in-law, short perhaps of the one thing he should have done, give up his daughter and let her be completely a wife. Short of that, he tried harder than most people would have done; unless there was an official banquet at Prime Minister's House, it was Nehru who moved to the side of the table, leaving Feroze the place at the head, and he was an admirable grandfather to the two boys. There was never a complete separation between Feroze and Indira; sometimes Feroze lived at the apartment allotted to him as a member of parliament, sometimes he lived at Prime Minister's House. To the end it was a marriage which, though not entirely successful, deeply involved the two people concerned. In the summer of 1960 they spent a month's holiday together in Kashmir—Kashmir, which keeps turning up in the story as a sort of Shangri-la for all of them. It has even been suggested that one of the reasons for Nehru's inability to cut through the Kashmir problem was that unconsciously he had buried his heart in that dream valley in the mountains and was unable to see straight; he admitted in his autobiography that he used to dream of Kashmir from inside the brick walls of prison compounds, saying to himself Walter de la Mare's lines :

> *Yea in my mind these mountains rise,*
> *Their perils dyed with evening's rose;*
> *And still my ghost sits at my eyes*
> *And thirsts for their untroubled snows.*

Not long after this Kashmiri holiday, Indira was in an airplane, flying home from Kerala, one of the problem states of India. Kerala's troubles have been many : shortage of food, Communist agitation, language riots. For whatever reason Indira had visited it, the visit had been a success, and coming back in the plane she was aware of a sense of elation and lightness of spirit, as though everything were for the best : "God's in his heaven : all's right with the world." Common sense pricked the bubble; she reminded herself that she never had this feeling without deflation following soon after.

The plane touched down at Delhi at eleven o'clock that night; people were waiting to take her at once to the hospital where Feroze had been admitted with a heart attack. She sat by his bed all night; he died in the morning.

An interesting comment on her life was made by the deaf Punjabi painter, Satish Gujeral, who came to Prime Minister's House early in 1956, commissioned to paint Nehru. In fact, Indira was the first to sit for him.

"Why do you wear a mask?" he said to her.

"You can't wear your heart on your sleeve all the time," she replied.

And he painted her as he saw her, as a refugee waif of the partition.

Then it was the Prime Minister's turn, and again Gujeral painted what he saw. In this picture Nehru is a dilettante figure; the familiar red rose in his buttonhole has turned pale green like Oscar Wilde's famous carnation; the background is burning, and over the man's shoulder there rises a sort of steel beetle skeleton, a symbol of conscience.

These two unlikely pictures hung in the conventional English surroundings of Prime Minister's House, which had been taken over as it stood from the British Commander-in-Chief in 1947. The pillared portico and handsome reception rooms opening into one another were suitable enough for the Indian as for the British raj, but the furnishings were incongruous for the new India. They were in English drawing-room style, all rosewood and flowered chintz.

If a house is the key to its inmates, over the next few years Prime Minister's House had much to tell. First it spoke of their relative poverty: even if Indira had wanted to make a clean sweep, she could not have afforded to. Her father's salary as Prime Minister was small; the royalties from his books were what kept the boys at school and the family afloat. They had nothing else to fall back on. Kamala's jewelry had all been sold to pay for Indira's studies abroad and for Kamala's long illness. Poverty, of course, is a relative term.

Compared with most people in India, the Nehrus lived
in luxury, but compared with the important foreigners
they had to visit abroad or entertain at home, they
were ridiculously poor. Never did a first lady wear
fewer decorations, and if Indira had hankered after the
trappings of her position—diamonds, for instance, or a
sable coat—she would have felt the pinch badly. Fortu-
nately, she preferred homespun cotton to any other
material—a very different thing, in its delicacy of
weave and color, from the rough *khadi* she had had to
wear as a child, about which she had complained to
Gandhi. Moreover, she looked superb in anything, and
had that enviable gift of making other women look
overdressed.

There was no point in discarding for the sake of
discarding, and so they lived in the Commander-in-
Chief's house with its pale-blue upholsteries like the set
for a drawing-room comedy of the English upper class.
Even the towels in the bathroom were remnants of the
British raj. Even if she could have afforded it, though,
perhaps Indira would not have known how to make the
place over to her own pattern; a friend has said that her
own room on the upper floor was never anything but a
nondescript bed-sitting room that might have been
anybody's lodgings in any country in the world.

Little by little, however, the East crept in to influence the conventional West, and the result was an odd
mixture. Though Indira might not be able to stamp a
whole house with her own image, she loved the arts of

many different cultures, and there was one good thing about tiresome state visits: at least one could pick up bits. Classical Chinese and Tibetan pieces found space in the great drawing-room, along with abstract paintings, Indian toys, a set of Alaskan Eskimo carvings. Her office was draped with Indian cottons of subtle color and design. And of course the official photographs silted up on every available surface. V.I.P.'s on visits to other V.I.P.'s always take their photographs for presentation, inscribed with illegible but very important signatures across the corner.

Indira seems never to have taken to public life at, so to speak, its private level. Probably, like her father, she happily drank the wine of adoration when it came from the great white crowds of peasant India. But at the level of state visits, and making conversation to diplomats and diplomats' wives, and arranging state dinners for special occasions, and working out protocol—no. She preferred to meet artists and creative people, to go out to dinner in some very small restaurant or go bargain hunting in the department stores to keep the boys in clothes. Her idea of happiness in Delhi was, at nightfall, to go out into the cool evening and walk barefoot on the damp grass, watching the clouds of parakeets screeching overhead to their roosting place.

At the same time, as many people found, she had the near-royal temperament of the Nehrus. Neither she nor her father suffered fools gladly, and with people who pretended too hard or flattered too much, or tried to

be what they were not, she could be both cold and
haughty and leave them floundering in their well-
meant politenesses.

It was 1956, and she was nearly forty, when she
took a real plunge into politics by becoming a member
of the Congress Working Committee, the policy-
making body. "Mrs. Gandhi may be a nice girl, but it
is only because she is the Prime Minister's daughter
that she is included on the Working Committee. She has
no qualifications in her own right. She has led a sheltered life," was the opinion of one informed source. But
then Delhi, like all capital cities, is full of informed
sources, and they contradict each other. It was true that
she had led a sheltered life; she was horrified by her
first gulp of political life—she had not expected the
double-think, the dishonesty, the pressurizing and corruption which she found behind the scenes, and she was
appalled by them. That sort of thing did not come near
Nehru, his integrity was too well known, and he tended
as he grew older to fend off unpleasant revelations and
trust people too much.

Three years later Indira, the third generation, was
elected president of Congress for a year. Watchers were
pleased to notice that she controlled sessions very well,
using the gavel as firmly on her father as on any other
long-winded member, but it cannot be said that she
showed any super-ability for the job. It was still the
same problem : no one could decide whether she had as
yet undeveloped potential, or whether, so to speak, all
her cards were on the table. Over and over again, as one

looks through newspaper files, one sees puzzled reporters trying to sum her up and confessing themselves unable to do it. The London *Times* in 1959 included her in a series of "People to Watch," but though the writer was quite sure she was worth watching and spent two informed columns saying so, he could not come to any conclusion about "this modest fastidious woman, the unobtrusive companion of her father's travels and associate of his labours."

Then, at the beginning of 1964, Jawaharlal was taken ill, and everybody knew for sure now that he was an old man, too old for the job he drove himself to carry out. Indira once more carried two burdens; at home she and the servant Nethu did all the nursing between them, but there was still her political work to be done, and meetings to be addressed. She looked exhausted, frozen, withdrawn further than ever behind her mask. And now the jockeying for position rose to new heights. In the event of the Prime Minister's death or incapacity, what was going to happen? Suddenly, not for the first time, Delhi buzzed with speculations about Indira's future. Perhaps after all she wanted to be Prime Minister herself. Perhaps she would find herself Prime Minister whether she wanted it or not. Or would she be satisfied with a lesser job, Foreign Minister perhaps? Who, in that case, would get her support as Prime Minister, support that was definitely worth having? The beehive was in turmoil.

Meanwhile, Nehru improved, but walked and spoke slowly, an old man. He was seventy-four, and it was plain that unless he retired and took things easy, his life was going to be short. "The last of the demigods," as someone called him, was flickering into his twilight. He did not retire and he did not take things easy. Four months later, on a May morning, he woke up with a pain in his back. It was a heart attack, and though there was time for six or seven doctors to arrive, they could not do anything useful. Jawaharlal Nehru was dead.

In India death is nearer to people than in Western countries. It is made sharply and terribly near by the Hindu custom of burning the body in front of its mourners. Perhaps because they believe in reincarnation they are able to stand this better than we could; the finality is only the finality of one life out of many; the great soul will return.

Even the most intimate mourning is terribly public. In the Indian heat (Delhi in May can experience temperatures well into the hundreds), there must be quick disposal of a body. Within two hours the public was filing through Jawaharlal's bedroom, while Indira, in the white sari that denotes mourning, sat according to custom on the floor beside the bed, and outside on the stairs and in the hall and on the lawn the question of the succession was thrashed out, openly or indirectly.

The whole of Delhi, it seemed, summoned by radio but still more quickly by the jungle telegraph which flickered at the speed of fire through the capital, surged toward Prime Minister's House, surged into the garden, and blocked all the surrounding streets until the police cordoned them off. The body was brought down to the verandah, where it lay between blocks of ice, propped up the better to be seen by the crowds, and wreathed with flowers. In no time there was a line two miles long in the hot sun, of people hoping to get near enough for a last look at that quiet face. Many noticed how in death his expression had settled into one of courage and resolution; in life his moods had varied so quickly that no expression had remained for long. The flowers tossed down by the crowds had to be constantly swept away like so much debris, or the pile would have covered him completely.

Next day at a conservative estimate two and a half million people gathered to watch the last procession through the streets. "They stood half a mile, a mile round in a vast silent circle as the procession rummaged through the crowded roads. It is a lake of people, white and cohesive." The body of Jawaharlal was to be burned on the flats of the Jumna River, very near the spot where, sixteen years before, the body of Gandhi had been burned. In his will Jawaharlal stated categorically that he did not want any religious ceremonies performed at his death: "I do not believe in any such ceremonies and to submit to them, even as a matter of form, would be hypocrisy and an attempt to delude ourselves and others."

His wishes were disregarded, as anyone might have foreseen. When a nation wants to mourn, it must be allowed to do so, and the object of its mourning belongs at that moment to the nation. One cannot imagine the

United States allowing itself to be deprived of the chance to mourn Kennedy, or Great Britain, Churchill. Nehru's body no longer belonged to the wishes of the dead Nehru. It belonged to India, to the huge, patient, white-clad crowds who lifted their children up for a last look at their leader.

The British Prime Minister chartered a Boeing 707 and flew in to see the last of the man whom his predecessors had so often put behind bars. With him came Mountbatten, last Viceroy and Nehru's personal friend. The Russians sent a deputy vice-premier. Other countries, those within reach, sent important representatives; except China, which sent a telegram of condolence so casual as to be insulting.

The heat that afternoon built up to 110 degrees, so that the red tika marks on women's foreheads melted in a sheen of sweat. The gun carriage drawn by ninety service men took three hours to make the five-mile journey.

At the end of it, the body of Jawaharlal Nehru, with a red rose in his buttonhole as he had always worn in life, was laid on the specially prepared platform, and then sticks and logs of sandalwood, soaked with butter, scattered with incense and sweet herbs, were piled higher and higher. Someone saw Indira, her face as white as the dead man's and drawn to a pinch of exhaustion, stumble down the three steps from the platform to join the crowd.

The priests chanted:

> *"Let your eye go to the sun,*
> *Your life to the wind,*
> *Turn to the waters if they draw you,*
> *Rest in the green plants . . ."*

Sanjay, Indira's younger son, a boy of seventeen, performed the last rites: crossed his grandfather's dead hands, tore the winding sheet, and plunged the flame among the logs of oil-soaked wood. A tongue of red flame, a wisp of black smoke, and then smoke and flame roared skyward for the waiting millions, that "lake of people," to see. This is the cruel consummation of a Hindu funeral, but it drains and purges grief.

"My desire to have a handful of my ashes thrown into the Ganga at Allahabad has no religious significance, so far as I am concerned . . . The Ganga has been to me a symbol and a memory of the past of India, running into the present, and flowing on to the great ocean of the future. And though I have discarded much of past tradition and custom, and am anxious that India should rid herself of all shackles that bind and constrain her and divide her people, and suppress vast numbers of them, and prevent the free development of the body and spirit; though I seek all this, yet I do not wish to cut myself off from that past completely. I am proud of that great inheritance that has been, and is, ours, and I am conscious that I too, like all of us, am a link in that unbroken chain which goes back to the dawn of history in the immemorial past of India. That chain I would not break, for I treasure it and seek inspiration from it. And as a witness of this desire of mine and as my last homage to India's cultural inheritance, I am making this request that a handful of my ashes be thrown into the Ganga at Allahabad to be carried to the great ocean that washes India's shore.

"The major portion of my ashes should, however, be disposed of otherwise. I want these to be carried high up into the air in an aeroplane and scattered from that height over the fields where the peasants of India toil, so that they might mingle with the dust and soil of India and become an indistinguishable part of India."

And so the second generation ended, leaving the third.

TWELVE

Madame Prime Minister

It did not escape anyone's notice on the afternoon of January 20, 1966, in the pillared central hall of the Parliament House in Delhi, that Indira Gandhi was wearing a red rose, as for years her father had worn one, fresh from the garden every day.

The voting was long and tedious. There were 530 Congress members present and each one had to be called from his seat, pick up his voting paper, go outside the chamber to mark it, and bring it back. It took four hours to work through the voting and another hour to count the ballot papers. There were many eyes on Indira, for at the end of all the ins and outs of intrigue which had followed Lal Bahadur Shastri's sudden death, it was well established that she would be chosen; the only thing that remained to discover was the margin of acceptance.

Although in Shastri's government she had accepted

137

nothing more important than the Ministry of Information and Broadcasting, she was at least now a knowledgeable member of a government. (Some people had thought that she might be made Foreign Minister, to use her considerable experience of the world outside India.) Nobody could accuse her now of being nothing but her father's housekeeper. The Indian scene had changed considerably since Nehru's death. If he had done nothing else, he had created an India which could accept Shastri as its premier, a small-town poor boy who had never stepped over India's frontier before becoming Prime Minister. More important still, he had left an India in which the president of Congress, Kumaraswami Kamaraj, was a black peasant from the south who spoke neither English nor Hindi. The United States has not yet got so far.

Now India was about to choose a woman prime minister. As the voting continued, people came and went and spoke to her, but from now on, in her white homespun sari and brown shawl, she would be confirmed in loneliness, in spite of, and because of, the seething busyness of her life.

What did it all amount to? Forty-eight years old, an orphan, and a widow. Her two sons, inheriting a dislike for the limelight, worked in England, one of them an engineering student, the other a working apprentice in the Rolls-Royce automobile plant. They would be lonely without her and she without them, but the choice was made and this was how it had to be. Perhaps there was really no choice. Given the powers behind her; given the fact that she was born into the middle of India's emergence into nationhood; given the people, Jawaharlal and Kamala, Motilal and Gandhi, Feroze and Tagore; given even the small circumstances—the little brother who died within a week, the policeman who carried furniture out of Anand Bhawan, the Moslem who nearly got lynched on the station platform; given all these things, the story seems to move like a well-conducted game of chess. Watching, you cannot see what the end of it will be, but you can see the logic of all the moves that have led up to this point.

The voting was conclusive, though not, as some people had hoped, unanimous. Indira Gandhi, 355 votes; Morarji Desai, her only rival, 169. It was not a surprise. A sharp-eyed reporter on his way to the parliament building had noticed that the chairs for the press conference were already arranged on the lawn of the small house where she lived with three servants and three dogs and no grandeur at all.

In her first speech she said: "My heart is full and I do not know how to thank you. I very well know we have many difficulties before us. But I also know that ours is a great country. As I stand before you, my thoughts go to the great leaders: Mahatma Gandhi, at whose feet I grew up; Panditji, my father; and Mr. Lal Bahadur Shastri . . . These leaders have shown us the way and I want to go along the same path. Mr. Lal Bahadur Shastri gave his life for peace. It should be our effort to advance the cause of peace and at the same time make the country strong and safeguard its security. I

have always regarded myself a servant of the nation
even as my father regarded himself as the first servant
of the nation . . .

"Ours is an ancient country with a great tradition
and heritage. There is something in this country which
enables its people, for all their illiteracy and backwardness, to rise to the occasion when face to face with
mighty challenges."

And perhaps she thought then of the verse which
Rabindranath Tagore had translated from the *Gitanjali*
and which Jawaharlal had quoted at the end of her
book, *Glimpses of World History*.

*Where the mind is without fear and the head is
held high;*
Where knowledge is free;
*Where the world has not been broken up into
fragments by narrow domestic walls;*
Where words come out from the depth of truth;
*Where tireless striving stretches its arms towards
perfection;*
*Where the clear stream of reason has not lost its
way into the dreary desert sand of dead habit;*
*Where the mind is led forward by Thee into ever-
widening thought and action—*
*Into that heaven of freedom, my Father, let my
country awake.*

A Brief Bibliography

Elmhirst, L. K.: *Sir Rabindranath Tagore, Pioneer in Education*. New York, Transatlantic Arts.

Fischer, Louis: *Gandhi*. New York, New American Library.

Gandhi, Mohandas K.: *Gandhi: An Autobiography*. Boston, Beacon Press.

Hutheesing, Krishna, ed.: *Nehru's Letters to His Sister*. London, Faber & Faber.

—: *With No Regrets*. London, Lindsay Drummond.

Lal, Ram Mohan: *Jawaharlal Nehru*. Allahabad, India.

Moraes, Frank: *Jawaharlal Nehru*. New York, Macmillan.

Mukherjee, H. M.: *Education for Fulness*. New York, Asia Publishing House.

Nanda, B. R.: *The Nehrus*. New York, John Day.

Nehru, Jawaharlal: *Autobiography*. New York, Paragon Book Gallery.

—: *A Bunch of Old Letters*. New York, Asia Publishing House.

—: *Conversations with Tibor Mende*. New York, George Braziller.

—: *The Discovery of India*. New York, Anchor Books.

141

——: *Glimpses of World History*. New York, John Day Co. Also available in condensed form in *Nehru on World History*, ed. by Saul K. Padover. New York, John Day.

——: *Independence and After*. New Delhi, Delhi Government Publications.

Norman, Dorothy, ed.: *Nehru: The First Sixty Years*. New York, John Day.

Also the archives of the British Broadcasting Corporation and *The Times* of London.

Index

143

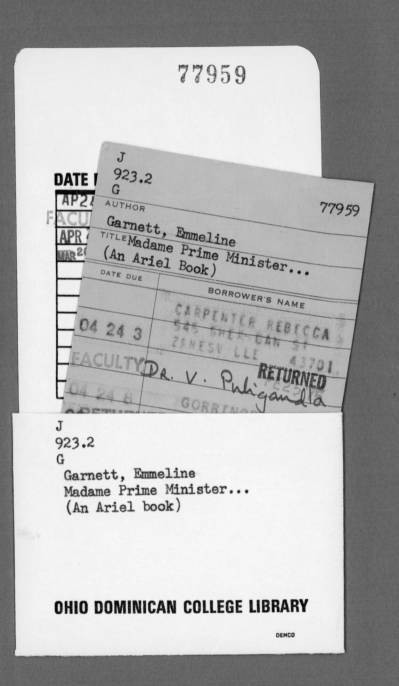